THE CHURCH
IN THE MOVEMENT
OF THE SPIRIT

The Church in the Movement of the Spirit

Edited by

William R. Barr and Rena M. Yocom

With a Foreword by

Michael Kinnamon

William B. Eerdmans Publishing Company
Grand Rapids, Michigan

Library of Congress Cataloging-in-Publication Data

The Church in the movement of the Spirit / edited by Wiliam R. Barr; with a foreword
   by Michael Kinnamon.
    p.   cm.
   Papers from a study group on ecclesiology and pneumatology of the Commission on
Faith and Order of the National Council of the Churches of Christ in the United
States of America.
  ISBN 0-8028-0554-X (pbk.)
   1. Holy Spirit. 2. Church. 3. Mission of the church. 4. Christian union. I. Barr,
William R., 1934-   . II. National Council of the Churches of Christ in the United
States of America. Commission on Faith and Order.
BT121.2.C48 1994
231'.3 — dc20   94-5572
                                                          CIP

Contents

Foreword   vii
Michael Kinnamon

Preface   ix
Clyde J. Steckel and Robert E. Hood

Introduction   1
William R. Barr and Rena M. Yocom

1   Biblical Basis and Guidelines   11
    Thaddeus D. Horgan, SA

2   Discerning the Spirit in the Life of the Church   29
    Cecil M. Robeck

3   The Spirit in the Worship and Liturgy of the Church .   51
    Lorelei F. Fuchs, SA, and Lawrence C. Brennan, C.M.

4   The Spirit in the Proclamation of the Church   75
    George Vandervelde and William R. Barr

5   The Spirit in the Formation and Forms of the Church   91
    William R. Barr and Horand Gutfeldt

6 The Spirit in the Ministry of the Church   111
    Rena M. Yocom

7 The Spirit in the Mission and Service of the Church   123
    Thomas Hoyt, Jr., and Clyde J. Steckel

Foreword

MICHAEL KINNAMON

After generations of relative neglect, the topic of the Holy Spirit is beginning to get the attention it deserves in ecumenical circles. This book is an important contribution to this developing conversation.

A major example of the new concern for our life in the Spirit was the Canberra Assembly of the World Council of Churches (1991) with its theme, "Come, Holy Spirit — Renew the Whole Creation." Reports from that assembly speak of a renewed longing for spiritual depth, especially in the West where it is increasingly clear that material well-being alone does not constitute life in its fullness. They also acknowledge that the entire earth is now threatened by the strife and pollution that mark so much of life on our planet. And along with this is an admission that our attempts to fix things are, by themselves, woefully inadequate. God alone is the source of creation. God alone can bind us together in the face of contentious differences. It is to God, ever present through the Holy Spirit, that we must attend if we would be united and renewed.

Something like this may have compelled the Working Group on Faith and Order of the National Council of Churches of Christ to undertake the study documented in this volume. While the chapters were written by various members of the commission, they are held together by a number of significant themes, including the following:

1. The Spirit is understood as "The One in whose power the church is one." This link between the Holy Spirit and Christian unity is not simply self-evident. Spirit-filled movements have often been regarded as more disruptive than unifying. This theme is important,

therefore, because it implies that authentic unity is inseparable from renewal in the ecumenical vision of the church.

2. There is an emphasis in the following pages on learning from Christians of other traditions how they experience the Holy Spirit moving in their worship, theology, mission, and decision-making structures. Indeed, the authors seem to be saying that we can speak about the presence of the Spirit precisely when our sense of mutual interdependence in the body of Christ is enhanced; when, to use Paul's language, the body is "built up" through the sharing of gifts. I am particularly grateful for the attention given to the witness of Pentecostals. This branch of the church has much to say about the working of the Spirit, but has too often been overlooked in ecumenical discussion.

3. These essays insist and demonstrate that "the Spirit delights in variety" while also probing the limits of acceptable diversity in the church. Christian community is diverse precisely because the Holy Spirit enables us to live beyond the tendency for "birds of a feather to flock together." But those who live in the Spirit are also empowered to struggle against the idolatries, the false diversities, that would enslave us.

4. The chapters that follow deal repeatedly with the sticky but crucial issue of discernment. What are the criteria for distinguishing the Holy Spirit from other spirits of the world, especially in this secularized and pluralistic age? I welcome the careful attention given to this question, a question that both dominated and disrupted the World Council's Canberra Assembly. I also welcome the emphasis on Scripture as a guide for discernment. These authors do not claim that Scripture tells us all we can know about the activity of God's Spirit; but they do suggest that the Bible must determine the direction of our search and thus curb the tendency to confuse the free-blowing Spirit with our wishful projections and ideological assumptions.

While I am pleased to commend all of the following essays, I want to take special note of the chapter by Thaddeus Horgan. It offers, for one thing, an admirable overview of biblical understandings of the Spirit. It is also, however, one of the last things written by an outstanding ecumenist. Fr. Horgan died in April of 1990, midway through this project, after a lifetime of dedicated service to the unity of Christ's church. Such commitment to wholeness is surely, itself, an indication of the movement of the Spirit.

Michael Kinnamon
Dean, Lexington Theological Seminary

Preface

CLYDE J. STECKEL AND ROBERT E. HOOD

Can a fresh look at the church in the movement of the Spirit and the experience of the Holy Spirit in the church make for greater Christian unity? "Not likely," might be the quick answer from some who are aware of the divisive effects of so-called spirit movements in the past and in more recent times.

But the authors of the essays in this volume beg to differ. Moreover, these essays reflect not only the views of their authors but also discussion across denominational lines that has occurred in a study group on the subject, convened as part of the Working Group on Faith and Order of the National Council of Churches, over the past four years. This group of persons from a wide variety of church traditions[1]

1. The members of the study group on Ecclesiology and Pneumatology included:

   Clyde J. Steckel, co-chair, United Church of Christ
   Robert E. Hood, co-chair, Episcopal Church
   Mortimer Arias, United Methodist Church
   William R. Barr, Christian Church (Disciples of Christ)

Clyde J. Steckel, professor of theology and psychology at the United Theological Seminary Twin Cities in Minneapolis, is a member of the United Church of Christ, and served on the earlier Faith and Order study of Dimensions of the Apostolic Faith.

Robert E. Hood, a representative of the Episcopal Church, serves as consultant for the Fund for Theological Education.

began by acknowledging that it seemed easier perhaps to accept other individual Christians as valued and valid members of the body of Christ and to recognize the Holy Spirit working in and through them than in the churches they represented and their relations. We then tried to examine whether the dynamics of the Spirit we discerned in Spirit-filled Christians might not lead us also to recognize more fully the movement of the Spirit in our own and other Christian churches, and enable them to receive one another more fully as truly branches of the church in a way that would draw us more closely together in Christ.

This study grew out of an earlier study of Faith and Order in which some of us shared, having to do with the expression and witness to apostolic faith in the North American context. The fruits of those labors were published in the volumes *Apostolic Faith in America,* edited by Thaddeus Horgan, SA, and a companion volume, *Black Witness to the Apostolic Faith,* edited by David T. Shannon and Gayraud S. Wilmore, both published by Eerdmans.[2] Our study group on the church and the Spirit (or, to use the more technical terminology, on Ecclesiology and Pneumatology), building on these prior studies, searched for commonalities and convergences, as well as learning from divergences, in our own and other traditions' experience of the Spirit.

In the effort to move forward in seeking a more united understand-

Emmanuel Clapsis, Greek Orthodox Archdiocese
Kyriaki FitzGerald, Greek Orthodox Archdiocese
Dean Freiday, Friends General Conference/Catholic & Quaker Studies
William E. Gordon, Jr., Southern Baptist Convention
Horand Gutfeldt, Swedenborgian Church
Thaddeus Horgan, Roman Catholic Church
Thomas Hoyt, Christian Methodist Episcopal Church
Winston Persaud, Evangelical Lutheran Church in America
Janet Pierce, Metropolitan Community Churches
Gilbert Stafford, Church of God (Anderson, IN)
George Vandervelde, Christian Reformed Church
Rena M. Yocom, United Methodist Church
Lynn E. Mitchell, Jr., Churches of Christ
Cecil M. Robeck, Assemblies of God
Jerry L. Sandidge, Society for Pentecostal Studies

2. Thaddeus D. Horgan, ed., *Apostolic Faith in America* (Grand Rapids, MI: Eerdmans, 1988); and David T. Shannon and Gayraud S. Wilmore, *Black Witness to the Apostolic Faith* (Indianapolis: Council on Christian Unity/Grand Rapids, MI: Eerdmans, 1985).

ing and witness to apostolic faith today, this quest kept running up against such questions as the authority of Scripture, the use of creeds and confessions, historic episcopacy, differences of polity, and the importance of personal experience of faith to which churches give different answers, and answers that are not readily harmonized. But we recognized that all our churches claim to give these answers by the leading of the one Spirit as well as the one Lord we confess. Would it be fruitful, then, to focus attention on the activity of the Holy Spirit in the church and to see if this might not shed some new light on issues blocking the way toward greater unity of the churches? After all, a common claim of the churches represented in the study group — which included mainstream member churches in the NCC, as well as representatives from the Roman Catholic Church, the Assemblies of God, the Church of God (Anderson, IN), Churches of Christ, Quakers, Swedenborgians, and Metropolitan Community Churches — was that the Holy Spirit is present and experienced in their faith and worship. Though representatives of the Eastern Orthodox Churches participated briefly in our discussions, we regret that they were unable to contribute an essay to this collection.

Our group was also diverse in gender, racial and ethnic composition, and sexual orientation. It included laypeople as well as ordained clergy. Members of the group whose essays and contributions to the study could not be included in this collection because of limitations of space nevertheless contributed important insights, raised helpful questions and criticisms, and made incisive suggestions as first and second drafts of the papers that form these chapters were discussed at semi-annual meetings of the study group from 1988 through 1991. In this discussion we ourselves experienced the leading of the Spirit as we struggled to grasp the meaning of ways of perceiving and speaking of the Spirit in other traditions, in theological perspectives different from our own, and in others' personal experiences of the Spirit.

Did we in fact make headway in gaining a new perspective on church-dividing issues by attending to the Spirit we all claim? We believe these essays will show that indeed we did. Not only did the trepidation about focusing on the Spirit felt by some members of the group abate considerably, but we also came to understand more deeply ways in which the Spirit gives life and nurtures it in our various Christian communions, in their worship, beliefs, patterns of church organization and decision-making, and in their communal and individual acts of mercy and justice-seeking.

At the same time we have come to realize that while the ecumenical movement both nationally and internationally has devoted much attention to doctrines of God and Christ as keys to Christian unity, relatively little attention has been given to the various churches' perceptions and living experiences of the Spirit in their traditions. But as we indicate here, it seems to us that to pursue this is also an important and promising avenue toward fuller Christian unity.

As the two members of the study group chosen to guide our deliberations and the discussions that produced these essays, we have discerned the Spirit working in wonderful and mysterious power in our midst to guide us and our churches to participate more fully in the Spirit's movement today. And we hope that through these essays the Spirit will also work to draw others more fully into its movement as they read and discuss these chapters.

We wish to express appreciation to Mrs. LaVerne Barnett of Lexington Theological Seminary for assistance in the production of this volume.

Introduction

WILLIAM R. BARR AND RENA M. YOCOM

The church is born in the movement of the Spirit. The Spirit's life-giving and transforming work includes the creation of a community of faith which bears witness to and serves as a means of the Spirit's ongoing activity. Furthermore, the church believes and experiences the Holy Spirit at work in its own life, empowering, nurturing, guiding, and renewing it in God's mission. But while the Spirit is active and manifested in the life of the church, the church does not control the Spirit. Rather, the presence and activity of the Spirit in the church is always a gift of God's free grace — for which the church prays, and which is always to be received with thanksgiving and joy. Further, the church has to acknowledge that the Spirit is not confined to the church. For, as Scripture attests and as the Spirit itself demonstrates, the Spirit is God's creative and redemptive, life-giving agency and power at work in the whole of creation, forming and transforming the world toward the fulfillment of God's aim.

Yet, surprisingly, the church has generally not given as much attention and study to the Holy Spirit and its role in the drama of redemption as it has to other aspects of Christian faith. The result of

---

William R. Barr, a member of the Christian Church (Disciples of Christ), teaches theology at Lexington Theological Seminary, Lexington, Kentucky.

Rena M. Yocom, a diaconal minister (permanent deacon), is the Associate General Secretary of the Mission Education and Cultivation Program department of the General Board of Global Ministries of The United Methodist Church.

1

this neglect has been a truncation of the church's witness and self-understanding as well as a diminishment of vitality. That is why we are concerned in this study to focus on the relationship of the Spirit to the church and to try to see more clearly how the Spirit works in the various facets of the life of the church. Our hope is that a deeper understanding of this will help the church manifest more clearly its life and unity in the Spirit.

The present study is part of a larger ongoing study in the NCCC's Faith and Order Working Group on the Apostolic Faith Today in the North American Context.[1] And this is itself part of a still wider study currently in process within the World Council of Churches, involving churches around the world, on seeking a "Common Expression of the Apostolic Faith Today."[2] It is hoped that as we find ways of giving a more united confession of our one faith, this, together with the statement on *Baptism, Eucharist and Ministry,* will help the churches move toward a fuller manifestation of their unity in Christ. It is within the context of this larger effort to give united expression to our shared faith that our study group has tried to see how a deeper understanding of the work of the Spirit in the church can contribute to a more united and effective witness to the gospel today.

We began by asking, Why is it that Christians often find it much easier to see and affirm the Spirit at work in the lives of individual persons than in the denominations and traditions to which these persons belong and in which they have been nurtured and shaped? For instance, why is it easier for us to discern the power of the Spirit at work in a Mother Teresa, a Martin Luther King, Jr., a Fannie Lou Hamer, an Oscar Romero, a Dorothy Day, a Lee Tai Young, a Billy Graham, a Millard Fuller, and a Desmond Tutu than in the various communions from which these persons come and in which they are actively involved? This obviously has ramifications also for our ecclesial communities in recognizing one another as authentically church and

---

1. Some of the results of the earlier phases of this study have been published in Thaddeus Horgan, ed., *Apostolic Faith in America* (Grand Rapids, MI: Eerdmans, 1988); and David T. Shannon and Gayraud S. Wilmore, eds., *Black Witness to the Apostolic Faith* (Grand Rapids, MI: Eerdmans, 1985).

2. See on this, Hans-George Link, ed., *Apostolic Faith Today: A Handbook for Study,* Faith and Order Paper No. 124 (Geneva: World Council of Churches, 1985); and *Confessing the One Faith,* Faith and Order Paper No. 153 (Geneva: World Council of Churches, 1991).

for joining together more fully in mission, service, and witness to the world. Our hope in pursuing a study of the church in the movement of the Spirit was not only to help one another see more clearly how the Spirit has been and is manifested in our own traditions but also to discern more clearly where the ongoing movement of the Spirit is leading the Christian community today.

Such recognition does not, however, come easily. It forces us to reexamine our various church traditions in the company of other streams of the Christian tradition. It requires us to dig deeply into the very heart of the faith we share. Ultimately it leads us to the most basic issue of all: the question of who and what is the Holy Spirit, and how is the Spirit's activity to be discerned in the church and in the world. This question is not only for professional theologians, but it must also concern each of us as we try to identify that which is at work among us giving and strengthening life and setting creation free. The question also arises amid the various and sometimes conflicting claims made about the Spirit and spirituality in our times. When is the Spirit truly manifested, and how is the Spirit active in the church and in the world?

As the church grapples with these questions it must draw upon the wisdom of all its members. More specifically, it must draw on what has been learned in all streams of the Christian tradition as well as from the promising convergence in understanding which is occurring through recent ecumenical dialogue.[3] However, it is not only through ecumenical conferences, papers, and scholarly discussion that we are led to a deeper and fuller understanding of the Spirit, but also increasingly today through peoples' experiences and their encounters in the global community.

Thus a study such as this must pay special attention to those voices which have often been neglected or suppressed, although we recognize we have not achieved this latter goal in the present study

3. As expressed, e.g., in the *Baptism, Eucharist and Ministry* statement, and in the significant Klingenthal Memorandum of 1979 which indicates significant convergence in Eastern and Western churches' understanding of the relation of the Spirit to the other members of the Trinity (the *filioque* issue); for the text of the Memorandum, see Link, *Apostolic Faith Today*, 231-44. For a discussion of the significance of the Memorandum, see S. Mark Heim and Theodore Stylianopoulos, eds., *Spirit of Truth: Ecumenical Perspectives on the Holy Spirit* (Brookline, MA: Holy Cross Orthodox Press, 1986).

to the extent we would have liked. Voices from other parts of the world, as well as from minorities in our midst, can teach us to think and speak of the Spirit more concretely in the struggle of people for justice and life.[4] These voices teach us to look for "the continuing empowerment of the spirit in our individual and social lives and in the larger economic and political world."[5] Many of these peoples who see the manifestation of the Spirit concretely in their ways of living with and relating to others speak of the Spirit eloquently through the use of images in songs, stories, and folk traditions.[6]

To speak of the Spirit as God's presence and life-giving and transforming activity in creation is to say something not only about what God *does* but also about who God *is*. That is, it is to make a statement about the divine identity, about the essential nature and character of God. For the Spirit of God (the phrase most commonly used in the Hebrew Scriptures; in the New Testament the Spirit is spoken of more frequently as the Holy Spirit) is not merely an effect of God but is God's own presence among us as the compassionate-passionate self-giving God.[7] Most of Christian tradition has imaged this in the doctrine of the Trinity, in which the Spirit is understood to be a distinctive and equal member of the triune community constitutive of God's being and life. As the Nicene-Constantinopolitan Creed of 381 puts it, the Spirit is "of the same being" *(homoousion)* with the other members of the Trinity. This is not merely a speculative statement but an acknowledgment that in the Spirit we are given life with God in the power of God. While this new life and the Spirit's clearest manifestation comes to us through Christ, the Spirit derives ultimately from the transcendent depths of God's being. As Emmanuel Clapsis has said, in a statement that reflects an Eastern Orthodox

4. See, e.g., J. Deotis Roberts, "The Holy Spirit and Liberation: A Black Perspective," in *Black Witness to the Apostolic Faith,* 50-62.

5. Mary Potter Engel and Susan Brooks Thistlethwaite, eds., *Lift Every Voice: Constructing Christian Theologies from the Underside* (San Francisco: Harper & Row, 1990), 12.

6. See, e.g., the essay by Rosemary Edet (Nigeria) and Bette Ebeya (Kenya) in *With Passion and Compassion: Third World Women Doing Theology,* ed. Virginia Fabella and Mercy Oduyoye (Maryknoll, NY: Orbis Books, 1988), 6ff.; also, C. S. Song, *Third-Eye Theology: Theology in Formation in Asian Settings,* rev. ed. (Maryknoll: Orbis Books, 1979, 1990), 4 *et passim.*

7. See, e.g., the insightful discussion of this by Rosemary Haughton, *The Passionate God* (New York: Paulist Press, 1981), 21ff.

perspective but that also expresses an emerging convergence in ecumenical thought, "In Trinitarian theology the Holy Spirit, although inseparably united to Jesus Christ, is not subsumed under him. On the contrary, there is a conscious effort to emphasize its distinctive roles as it relates to Jesus Christ within God's salvific economy."[8] The author goes on to point out that among the distinctive roles or activities of the Spirit are the creating and building up of the church, uniting believers in a vital communion *(koinōnia)*, guiding and empowering the church in worship and service, maintaining the "consistency" of the church through different times and situations, relating the church to God's wider activity in the world, and giving a foretaste of the future toward which God calls and leads us.

Ecumenical study of the Spirit is leading us to deeper insights into the movement of the Spirit in the world and in the church. It is also leading us to a deeper understanding of the communion/community of the members of the Trinity and the significance of the Trinity as God's life in community for the kind of community of equality, justice, and love to which God calls us, and of which the church is called to be both a sign and a sacrament.[9]

These insights have been deepened and enlarged through our study of the Spirit in the life and mission of the church. We have come to see more clearly that the source and power of the church's life is the work of the Holy Spirit, that its life is to be shaped in and by the Spirit, and that the church is to live and pray in daily expectation of the Spirit. We have come to recognize more fully that essential to apostolic faith and our common confession of and witness to it is a fuller and deeper life in the Spirit. As we have shared with each other perceptions of the Spirit from our various traditions, we have also been led to a clearer discernment of the Spirit and its working in the whole course of the Christian tradition. We offer here some of the fruits of this study in the hope that this may be of help to others in seeking to discern more clearly and to live more fully in the ongoing movement of God's Spirit.

Our study begins with a review of biblical foundations and guide-

---

8. Emmanuel Clapsis, "The Holy Spirit in the Church," *Ecumenical Review* 41 (July 1989): 339.

9. For more on this, see Günther Gassmann, "The Church as Sacrament, Sign and Instrument," in *Church, Kingdom, World: The Church as Mystery and Prophetic Sign,* ed. Gennadios Limouris, Faith and Order Paper No. 130 (Geneva: World Council of Churches, 1986).

lines for discerning and understanding the Spirit. The late Thaddeus Horgan, who played a leading role in the early stages of this study, shows in his essay the important and decisive role of the Spirit in God's salvific activity as attested in Scripture. While he points out that Scripture does not present a fully developed doctrine of the Spirit, he shows that Scripture nevertheless clearly and powerfully attests to the experience of the Spirit and its role in creating, sustaining, and guiding the church. The discussion focuses on some key images of the Spirit and their meaning within the biblical narrative. But in the concluding sections of the chapter attention is given also to how the biblical witness to the Spirit can inform our understanding and discernment of the Spirit in the church today. Here the point is emphasized that the biblical testimony is at once both a source of guidance and a call to the church today to show forth in all aspects of its life that it lives in the power of the life-giving and sustaining Spirit of God.

The scriptural witness to the Spirit provides the foundation on which further understanding of the Spirit can be developed, as occurs later, for instance, in the Nicene Creed, the Reformation confessions, the experience of the Spirit in Anabaptist, Quaker, Pietist, Holiness, Pentecostal, and more recent charismatic movements, and in experiences of the Spirit around the world today in breaking down barriers of division, injustice, and discrimination, and in calling us all to greater ecological responsibility.[10]

On the basis and in the light of the scriptural testimony to the Spirit, the church today must attempt rightly to discern the Spirit as experienced and active in its midst. Mel Robeck argues that not all claims concerning the Spirit and/or inspiration of the Spirit should be taken at face value; but rather such claims have to be carefully examined and tested as we seek to discern the Spirit in the life of the church. Robeck identifies several biblical tests which provide criteria for discerning the activity of the Spirit among us and in the church. Yet ultimately, he suggests, it is not the church that defines the Spirit but rather the Spirit that defines the church. This has to be the case since it is the Spirit that creates the church and that works to shape the church to serve faithfully in God's mission.

---

10. See Emilio Castro, ed., *To the Wind of God's Spirit* (Geneva: World Council of Churches, 1990), consisting of selected essays on the theme from *The Ecumenical Review* in preparation for the Canberra Assembly of the World Council of Churches.

Succeeding chapters then explore the discernment and work of the Spirit in various facets of the church's life. In their essays on the work of the Spirit in the worship of the church, and more particularly in the liturgy, Sr. Lorelei Fuchs and Fr. Larry Brennan begin by clarifying the distinction between worship and liturgy, then go on to trace the development of understanding and practice of liturgical renewal within recent Roman Catholic tradition, and conclude with a discussion of the biblical foundations for a clearer understanding of the activity of the Spirit in the church's worship. This reflection also recognizes that various traditions use the terms *worship* and *liturgy* somewhat differently and suggests that these differences also can contribute to a fuller understanding and practice of worship in the power of the Spirit.

In the following chapter, George Vandervelde and William Barr focus attention on the work of the Spirit in the proclamation of the church. They point out that in one sense the whole life of the church is proclamation of the gospel. But in another sense the proclamation of the church, in the narrower meaning of the term, is its specific articulation of the gospel. Here the Spirit is active not only in *what* the church says, i.e., the content of its proclamation, but also in the power and effectiveness of its proclamation. The Spirit manifests itself in making the word of proclamation life-changing and unifying not only in the lives of persons but also in the life of the churches, and in their relations.

Perhaps less obvious is that the Spirit is also at work in the formation and forms of the church — in its order, structure, procedures, and decision-making. This is examined in Chapter Five, first through a series of brief case studies of how the Spirit is perceived as working in and through the organization of the church in some older and some more recent church traditions. Here the relation of the Spirit to issues of governance, discipline, authority, freedom, and decision-making and implementation is considered. The discussion then moves to some observations and reflections on the work of the Spirit in the varied patterns of church life. Through all these varied forms we nevertheless discern that it is the same Spirit at work ministering in various ways to the varied needs of people. Yet this variety of church structures and ways of decision-making also raises critical questions concerning where and how the Spirit is at work through them. Some ways of testing church structures in and by the Spirit are then considered. While it has to be recognized that the Spirit both uses and judges such structures, it is certainly the case that the Spirit is not manifested unambiguously in the organization of the church and its functioning. We have to recognize that, in fact, there may be in these structures resistance to the movement of the Spirit through clinging to forms that discriminate and that deny people full participation in the life of the church. Yet the Spirit cannot forever be quenched; it breaks through in surprising new ways and again and again raises up prophetic voices to challenge and guide the church in its continuing journey.

Very important in this regard is the Spirit's work to generate and empower the ministry of the church: first of all the ministry of the whole church, of all its members, and also that of its representative, ordained ministry, whose ministry must be understood and exercised within the ministry of the whole people of God. Rena Yocom points out that the invocation of the Spirit (*epiclesis*) and the laying on of hands in ordination become instruments and symbols for the ordinand's new Spirit-filled life and work. She also points out that the Spirit works before and beyond these means in the calling, education, examination, and nurture of those who are called to ordained ministry.

Yet the ministry of the church in the power and movement of the Spirit must be directed not only inward to the community of faith but also outward to the world — in outreach, service, and mission. The concluding essay by Thomas Hoyt and Clyde Steckel explores this dimension of the Spirit's activity in and through the church. Hoyt shows that in the biblical picture the church is created in the movement of the Spirit toward the neighbor. The Spirit that filled Jesus and that is communicated to his followers is the Spirit that sends the church to proclaim release to the captives, good news to the poor, and liberation to the oppressed. Steckel follows up on this by underscoring that the church is called to a "servant ministry," which necessarily today takes a variety of forms. These servant ministries are more than simply humanitarian acts of concern and help to those in need; they become channels through which the Spirit works to free, empower, and assist those with whom the church serves to create a community of justice and compassion. The chapter concludes by showing how a greater receptivity to the leading of the Spirit can be helpful in recognizing and appreciating both general and specific gifts of service, in overcoming the conflict between ministries of personal care and social justice, and in the empowering of servant ministries.

Readers may not agree with all the ideas concerning the Spirit expressed in these pages; members of the study group did not agree completely with all these views, drawn from different church traditions and perspectives. But we did believe it important to listen carefully to these different views of the Spirit's activity in the church and to try to discern what the Spirit might teach us through these different perspectives.

Our study began in prayer and appeal to the Holy Spirit for guidance and enlightenment, and it concludes also in prayer and appeal for the continuing work of the Spirit: *Veni, spiritus sancti* — Come, Holy Spirit, renew the church and the whole of creation!

Chapter One

Biblical Basis and Guidelines

THADDEUS D. HORGAN, SA

For all Christians the sacred Scriptures which are transmitted, read and interpreted in the church are acknowledged as normative for understanding our shared faith. To be sure, Scripture is read and understood in quite different ways within the church and among the churches, and this is especially so today.[1] Yet in recent biblical study attention is focused increasingly on the narrative structure, unity and power of the text in and through which God's Word comes to us.[2] As we

---

1. See, *inter alia*, Kenneth Hagen et al., *The Bible in the Churches: How Different Christians Interpret the Scriptures* (New York: Paulist Press, 1985); Stephen Breck Reid, *Experience and Tradition: A Primer in Black Biblical Hermeneutics* (Nashville: Abingdon, 1990); Donald K. McKim, *A Guide to Contemporary Hermeneutics* (Grand Rapids, MI: Eerdmans, 1986); Letty Russell, ed., *Feminist Interpretation of the Bible* (Philadelphia: Westminster Press, 1985); John Breck, *The Power of the Word* (Crestwood, NY: St. Vladimir's Seminary Press, 1986); Joseph Ratzinger et al., *Biblical Interpretation in Crisis* (Grand Rapids, MI: Eerdmans, 1989); Mark Lau Branson and C. Rene Padilla, eds., *Conflict and Context: Hermeneutics in the Americas* (Grand Rapids, MI: Eerdmans, 1986); and R. S. Sugartharajah, ed., *Voices from the Margin: Interpreting the Bible in the Third World* (Maryknoll, NY: Orbis Books, 1991).

2. See, e.g., Robert Alter, *The Art of Biblical Narrative* (New York: Basic Books,

---

The late Thaddeus Horgan, SA, was Associate Director of the Bishops' Committee for Ecumenical and Interreligious Affairs of the National Conference of Catholic Bishops. He edited the volume *Apostolic Faith in America,* which grew out of the Apostolic Faith Study of the Faith and Order Working Group in the prior triennium.

undertake a study of the Spirit, we should, therefore, listen anew and carefully to this narrative and be responsive to the guidance it gives as we seek a deeper understanding of the work of the Spirit in the various facets of the church's life.

But it is important to be clear at the outset concerning just what it is Scripture presents us with in this regard. It does not provide us with a fully developed, detailed doctrine of the Spirit. Rather, in the course of the biblical narrative we encounter a number of key themes, images, and indications of experience of the Spirit. These recurring themes and images concerning the Spirit can serve to challenge and guide the church in formulating a theology of the Spirit and in the further critical development of such a theology. Moreover, we need to note that Scripture both speaks *about* the Spirit and *is also itself a work of the Spirit,* not only in inspiring and guiding the writers but also at work in their readers and hearers helping us discern and appropriate the truth they proclaim (see, for example, 1 Cor. 2:6-15; John 16:14; 1 Pet. 1:10-12). Therefore, we must pay attention not only to what Scripture says *about* the Spirit but also to how Scripture conveys and serves the ongoing work of the Spirit.

First, then, let us consider what Scripture says concerning the Spirit. What we notice immediately is that Scripture does not describe the Spirit in itself but rather speaks of the Spirit only within the context of God's creative-redemptive relation to the world. While many things can be said about the "mystery" of the divine activity, nothing brings this to the fore more than a focus on the Spirit who works in and through the entanglements of the human journey to effect God's creative and re-creative mission and to bring people to fullness of life in communion with God.

From the Scriptures we learn that it is the will of the triune God to create and recreate humanity and to draw all into the people of God (Isa. 49:6; 1 Pet. 2:9-10), to unite all in the body of Christ, and that God works to implement this aim through the Spirit (cf. Gen. 1:2; 2:7; Isa. 11:1-9; John 14:26; etc.). God's Spirit, which has been active from the beginning of creation and which again and again raised

---

1981); also, Mark Ellingsen, *The Integrity of Biblical Narrative* (Minneapolis: Fortress Press, 1990); Edgar V. McKnight, *The Bible and the Reader: An Introduction to Literary Criticism* (Philadelphia: Fortress Press, 1985); and idem, *Postmodern Use of the Bible* (Nashville: Abingdon Press, 1988).

up leaders for God's people, is portrayed as having powerfully engendered Jesus Christ as Emmanuel, "God with us," as the primal sacrament of God's presence in the world (Matt. 1:23; John 1:1-14). Furthermore, Jesus is portrayed as having carried out his ministry of liberation and redemption, culminating in his death and resurrection, in the power of the Spirit (as the baptismal accounts in the Synoptic Gospels clearly indicate: cf. Mark 1:10 par.). But it was above all the gift of the Holy Spirit at Pentecost that gave birth to the church and that empowers it to share in God's mission (Acts 2:1-4). It is the Spirit that makes the church the sacramental presence of Christ and the sacrament of humanity's union with God in God's grace. And it is the Spirit that blesses, transforms, enlivens, and uses the gifts of all the members of the church to share in God's world-redeeming mission (1 Cor. 12:4ff.). Even more, the presence of the Spirit is depicted as a foretaste of the fullness of life with God which is the essence of Christian hope (2 Cor. 1:22 and 5:5). This gives a brief overview of the presentation of the Spirit in the biblical story. We will now look more closely at some of the basic elements in the biblical presentation of the Spirit.

But before we do so, it may be well to make a historical observation in the light of the biblical depiction of the Spirit. In Western church traditions, theological reflection on the Spirit, which is often referred to more technically as pneumatology, has generally been more Christ-centered and church-centered than centered on the Spirit in its own identity and distinctiveness. Eastern Christian tradition, on the other hand, has emphasized the distinctiveness of the Spirit and maintained the ancient focus on the Spirit in a doxological context. At the same time, the writings and soteriological interests of Eastern theologians of the early period show that they too were concerned to understand rightly the relation of the Spirit to Christ and within the Trinity. In the modern ecumenical movement, the increasing dialogue between Western and Eastern churches, as well as with traditions from other parts of the world church, is leading all these traditions toward a richer understanding of the Spirit, not only as active in the present but also as attested in the biblical narrative.

The Spirit in the Hebrew Scriptures

The Spirit that is bestowed upon Jesus in his baptism and that is active in and through him is continuous with the Spirit of God attested in Israel's Scriptures. It is through Israel's witness that we come to see more clearly that God is active in the world through the agency of the Spirit. The Hebrew term for spirit, *ruach,* translated as *pneuma* in Greek, literally means a movement of air, and the power creating that movement. It can mean a gentle breeze or a strong wind; yet the same term also is used to refer to breath, the "breath of life" (e.g., Gen. 7; Wis. 15:11), as well as to the extraordinary power which at certain times "falls upon" and is manifested through some people (1 Sam. 10:6, 10). It is God's Spirit or *ruach* that gives life and is the power of life. But it is also this same Spirit that in some situations gives extraordinary power, as when people such as Gideon and Deborah are called to do mighty deeds in the service of God. God's Spirit is said to have "fallen" or "rushed" on Samson, Samuel, and David. But this extraordinary endowment of the Spirit is depicted not as a permanent gift but as a temporary empowerment limited to particular occasions when its recipients were called to be instruments of God's deeds of deliverance of Israel.[3]

Prophecy, in ancient times, was sometimes seen as resulting from possession by God's Spirit (cf. 1 Sam. 10:6, 10; 16:13). Yet the inspiration of the great prophets is not ascribed to the work of the Spirit so much as to a direct encounter with "the word of the Lord."[4] This divine action is said in some texts to have been followed by the gift of the Spirit (e.g., 1 Sam. 16:13; 2 Esdr. 14:22). Also, at times the gift or anointing of the Spirit is referred to in connection with the empowerment of the righteous king. It is this that enables the king

---

3. See L. A. Bushinski, "Spirit of God," *New Catholic Encyclopedia,* 1st ed. See also Baumgartel, "Spirit in the Old Testament," and Bieder, "Spirit in Judaism," s.v. "pneuma," in *Theological Dictionary of the New Testament,* ed. Gerhard Friedrich (Grand Rapids, MI: Eerdmans, 1968), VI:359-389. But for a view emphasizing the continuing charismatic activity of the Spirit in Israel's leaders, see Leon J. Wood, *The Holy Spirit in the Old Testament* (Grand Rapids, MI: Zondervan, 1976).

4. See Gerhard von Rad's statement that, except for the account of the transfer of Elijah's *charisma* to Elisha in 2 Kings 2:15, "the prophets from Amos onwards do not think of themselves as bearers of the Spirit, but as preachers of the word of Jahweh." *Old Testament Theology,* trans. D. M. G. Stalker (New York: Harper & Row, 1965), 2:56f.

to be just and fair, to save the poor, and to defend the oppressed (Isa. 11:2-4). The Spirit is presented as working through the king to create a community which is to be both a witness to and the sign of God's rule.

Furthermore, in Isaiah 42:1-4 and 61:1ff., the Spirit of God empowers the "servant of Yahweh" (meaning Israel? the remnant? a prophet? a coming messianic figure?) to bring justice to the nations and to proclaim God's jubilee of grace and peace, or *shalom*.

Finally, we should note that the "pouring out of the Spirit," not only on Israel but "on all flesh" (Joel 2:28-29), is seen as the decisive sign and completion of God's redemptive work.

In summary, then, it can be said that in the Hebrew Scriptures God's Spirit is presented as acting in creation, in raising up leaders of Israel, in connection with the prophets, and as the power and sign of the fulfillment of God's mission.

At the same time the same term refers to the human spirit as the "breath of life" given from God, which manifests itself in a person's character and behavior and relationships (e.g., Ezek. 36:26-27; Ps. 51:10; Wis. 7:7). Here the term is closely related to the Hebrew term for "heart," the seat of emotion, or as we might put it today, the depths and center of human personality, that which is constitutive of selfhood. The term thus also includes the decision-making activity of human being, not only individually but also corporately. It is God's Spirit that enables the human spirit to act in accordance with the divine will. The passage in Ezekiel referred to above envisions not only individuals but the people as a whole empowered by the Spirit to live out God's purpose. And this vision of a Spirit-filled people responsive to God's will is a theme that continues from the Hebrew into the Christian Scriptures.

The Spirit and the Word Made Flesh

In the Gospels the representation of the Spirit is connected inseparably with Christ. The Spirit, though distinctive in its own identity and activity, is nevertheless not independent of Christ but is closely conjoined with the person, work, and mission of Christ. Yet Jesus is depicted as both receiver and sender of the Holy Spirit (cf. Mark 1:10 par. with Jesus' promise of the Spirit in John 14–16). It is by the

power of the Spirit that Mary conceives and gives birth to Jesus (Matt.
1:18). At his baptism Jesus receives the Spirit, and exercises his ministry
in the power of the Spirit. Mark is even bold enough to say that the
Spirit "drove" Jesus into the wilderness for his first struggle with and
rejection of Satan (Mark 1:12-13).

In the Johannine community, as reflected in the Gospel of John
and the Johannine epistles, the great concern is to proclaim that in Jesus
Christ God's love has broken through the power of darkness pervading
the world and gives to those who believe in Christ eternal life. Here the
Spirit is spoken of primarily as that which communicates to believers
the eternal life, light, and truth given in Christ. This is why John's
Gospel emphasizes Jesus' statement about the necessity of being "born
anew by water and the Spirit" to receive the life God gives (John 3:5).
This is followed in John's Gospel by accounts of the seven messianic
signs Jesus performed, which reveal not only his divine power and
authority but also the meaning of his death and resurrection (which are
synthesized in John's account). The Spirit serves to bring into clear
focus Jesus' identity and the meaning of his activity. But the Spirit also
signifies the power the risen Lord communicates to his disciples to bear
witness to him. Fr. Raymond Brown speaks of the disciples' witness as
"simply the exteriorization of the Spirit's witness."[5]

The Synoptic Gospels, however, are more concerned with proclaiming Jesus as the messenger of God who is filled with charismatic
power. They relate Jesus' public ministry as activity in which the Spirit
is the enabling power: in his preaching, teaching, delivering, and
healing (see, for example, Matt. 12:28; Mark 3:29). In the Gospel of
Luke Jesus is presented as announcing in his first sermon the fulfillment
of Isaiah's prophecy concerning the anointing of the Spirit (Isa.
61:1ff.) in him and his work of setting free the oppressed and announcing the advent of God's reign (Luke 4:18-19). Jesus is also said
to have "rejoiced in the Spirit" (Luke 10:21) and to have promised
that God would give the Holy Spirit to those who sincerely asked for
it (Luke 11:13). Empowered by the Spirit, Jesus worked healing acts
that were signs of the transforming power of the coming *basileia* of

---

5. Raymond E. Brown, S.S., *The Gospel According to John,* The Anchor Bible,
Vol. 29 (Garden City, NY: Doubleday, 1966), 3:690, 698-701. See also Gary M. Burge,
·*The Anointed Community: The Holy Spirit in the Johannine Tradition* (Grand Rapids,
MI: Eerdmans, 1986), chap. 5.

God (Luke 4:1, 14). The activity of the Spirit is especially prominent in the Lukan texts (see, for example, Luke 1:15, 17, 35, 41, 67; 2:25, 26; 4:1, 14; 10:21; Acts 1:2, 5, 8; 2:4, 38; 4:8, 31; 6:5; 7:55; 8:29; 10:38; etc.). Luke underscores the presence and action of the Spirit not only in Jesus but also in the life of the church.

In the Gospels, Jesus not only encourages his followers with the assurance that the Spirit will strengthen them for resolute witness to the gospel but he also suggests that the Spirit will teach them what to say (Luke 12:11-12) and will guide them into all the truth (John 16:12-15). Further, as the risen Lord, he is said to have continued to instruct the apostles "through the Holy Spirit" (Acts 1:2) and promised that by the power of the Holy Spirit they would be his witnesses to the ends of the earth (Acts 1:8). In the Gospel of John, after his resurrection Jesus is presented as breathing "the Spirit of truth" on his followers (John 20:22-23), empowering them to forgive sins. And finally, in Matthew's account, the risen Christ commands his apostles to go and make disciples, baptizing them "in the name of the Father, and of the Son and of the Holy Spirit" (Matt. 28:18-20).

Thus, even as Jesus receives the Spirit in the Gospels' portrayal, he also communicates the Spirit to the church to guide and empower the church in carrying out its ministry. In the Gospel of John Jesus is represented as promising the coming of the Spirit as the Paraclete, meaning advocate or defender of the truth, who will "witness on my behalf" (John 15:16-26). To "witness" is, in the context of the Gospels, not only to preach the good news but also to give testimony to the truth by word and deed, even if need be to the point of martyrdom. At Pentecost the apostles and disciples are endowed and "filled with the Spirit" (Acts 2:4). They can now carry out their mission because they are moved by the same Spirit that was active in Jesus, which is able to break Satan's grip on the world and heal the wounded creation. This clearly indicates that the church does not live only out of its own human resources. Its true power is the power that comes from the Spirit active in and through it, which also acts in judgment and renewal of its own life (Rev. 2–4).

Jesus promises that his followers will be energized by his own charismatic power. But the possession of such power — or rather, the being possessed by it — is not something to be taken for granted, nor something which is under our control. The authentic sign of its presence is, as in Jesus himself, the willingness to be faithful in witness to God even unto death. The passions of both Stephen and Paul, as well as of many faithful martyrs since, demonstrate this point. But such acts of self-sacrifice also remind us that the calling of every Christian is to be faithful unto death, and that this is possible only in the power of the Spirit (see, for example, 1 Cor. 12:3; Gal. 5:5).

The Spirit and the Church

In the biblical narrative the Holy Spirit is portrayed as generating and upbuilding the church. The early Christian community, from its beginnings within Judaism and its later rapid spread through the larger Hellenistic world, drew adherents largely from the poor and marginalized (although some persons of wealth and prominence were also drawn to the new movement, such as Lydia). The rise and spread of the Christian movement must be understood within its social context, its "social world"; and it shares some characteristics of other social movements of its time.[6] Yet, as Schillebeeckx points out, such analyses cannot give a wholly adequate explanation of the Christian movement, for these communities drew not only on their own resources and those of their environment but they were communities, as Scripture attests, "living from the Spirit" and witnessing in its power.[7]

The activity of the Spirit in the church is manifested first of all in confirming the apostolic preaching and making it effective in the life of the community (see 1 Thess. 1:4-6; Rom. 8:9-11). This stands at the head of the list of characteristics of the church that the apostolic community preserved. Moved and formed in the Spirit, the church is called to faithfulness to the mission given it in God's ongoing work; and as it does so it becomes an efficacious sign of the coming of God's reign. In this community there are to be no aliens (Eph. 4:11-22) and no discrimination (Gal. 3:28), for all have been reconciled and made one in Christ. They are all God's children, "born of water and the

6. See, e.g., Howard Clark Kee, *Christian Origins in Sociological Perspective* (Philadelphia: Westminster Press, 1980); John G. Gager, *Kingdom and Community: The Social World of Early Christianity* (Englewood Cliffs, NJ: Prentice-Hall, 1975); and Gerd Theissen, *Sociology of Early Palestinian Christianity* (Philadelphia: Fortress Press, 1978).

7. Edward Schillebeeckx, *The Church with a Human Face,* trans. John Bowden (New York: Crossroad, 1990), 34-39.

Spirit" (John 3:5). The Holy Spirit is the dynamic principle of their life, both individually and corporately (2 Cor. 3:1-6; Phil. 1:19; Titus 3:4-7). Not only does the apostolic word proclaim this, but the movement of the Spirit effectively demonstrates it in the life and witness of the community. Indeed, it is the Spirit that empowers persons to respond to the proclamation with the confession that "Jesus is Lord." For, says Paul, no one can truly make this confession except as moved by the Holy Spirit (1 Cor. 12:3).

But such proclamation occurs in and through the Christian community, the church, as Christ's "body." Thus the Spirit's activity in empowering the proclamation of the Word and generating faithful response to it is not separate from but is integral to its work of forming the whole of the church's life as the body of Christ. In the church the faithful are bound together in "one spirit with him" (1 Cor. 6:17-20) because they are filled with the one Spirit (Rom. 8:9) and through baptism are made one in Christ. The Spirit dwells in each one, and in the church as a whole (1 Cor. 3:16-17; 6:19-20). It is this that bonds them together in Christ and that is to be manifested in their life. But this is itself even at its best only a foretaste, an appetizer, as it were, of the eschatological fullness of salvation which God promises in Christ and through the Spirit (Rom. 8:23; 2 Cor. 1:22; 5:5). This is concretely and centrally manifested in the eucharist, which is both the celebration of what God has given us in Christ and the anticipation of the fullness of salvation in God's future (1 Cor. 11:26).

The transformation of life effected in and by the Spirit is what Scripture refers to as "sanctification." In our finite grasp of this it is only possible to express what this means through a series of phrases or images which even then do not fully capture the depth and extent of the life-transforming change the Spirit works in and through the church. For instance, Scripture speaks of this in terms of the Spirit's exposing (throwing light on) the sins of the world, of leading people to ask God's forgiveness and truly repenting, of enabling people to turn in forgiveness, love, compassion, and service to their neighbor, of coming to ever fuller knowledge of the truth, of becoming a more faithful servant of the living God, and of exercising the gifts of ministry "bestowed on us by God" (1 Cor. 12:4ff.).

All of this is concretely focused in the biblical narrative in the account of the descent of the Spirit on the apostles, Mary, and the other disciples at Pentecost (Acts 2:2-3), which gives birth to the church and empowers it for witness and service. This service is nothing other than advancing the gospel. The Spirit turned first Peter, and then the other apostles and disciples, outward to the world and enabled them to proclaim the good news of God's redemption in Jesus Christ. Peter recognized in the Spirit's power manifested among them the fulfillment (or at least the beginning fulfillment) of the prophecy in Joel, that God would pour out the Spirit on all flesh (Acts 2:14-39). The church is created to serve and witness in God's ongoing mission in the movement of the Spirit. Empowered and guided by the Spirit, the church's vision is continually expanded and her life enriched by the entrance of new peoples into the community of faith (as the opening chapters of Acts so powerfully attest). This is supported by the clarion call in the Pauline letters summoning all the members of the church to bear witness to the gospel and to preserve their unity in Christ (1 Cor. 12:11-13). Such unity is not simply to be enjoyed for its own sake but it is also so that the world may believe (John 17:23). In other words, so that the church's witness will have credibility because it lives in the power of the gospel it attests.

Still, it is true that the church, too, struggles to overcome legacies of prejudice, discrimination, and separation within its own life. The Spirit both guides and judges the church in this struggle (Rom. 8:4-11). For the church today to address issues of racism, sexism, classism, and ageism within the church as well as in society is not extraneous to the church's witness to the gospel but integral to its proclamation. In this process, painful as it may be, the Spirit is working to teach, correct, and transform the church (1 Pet. 4:17) as well as the world. We must learn to hear and respond to the Spirit's working through those who have been ignored and marginalized for too long in the church's journey. Through them the Spirit is speaking urgently in and to the church today.[8]

What the biblical narrative makes quite clear is that the church is a communion in the Holy Spirit which breaks down all humanly erected divisions. It is a community in which all are equally God's children, even though its members have different gifts of service. All are sisters and brothers in Christ, who hold to the teaching of the

8. See, e.g., Susan Brooks Thistlethwaite and Mary Potter Engel, eds., *Lift Every Voice: Contructing Christian Theologies from the Underside* (San Francisco: Harper & Row, 1990).

apostles, to the "breaking of bread," to care for and communion with others, and to prayer in which God's love and power are received and shared (Acts 2:42-47). In the church, through the presence and work of the Holy Spirit, we are to become what God has made us in Christ, namely, "partakers of the divine nature" (John 17:22, 26). Membership in the church is not therefore incidental nor secondary to life in the Spirit — whatever one may hear otherwise amid the variety of claims to the Spirit on the current scene. The Spirit gathers people into the community of faith, forms and reforms this community in its journey, and works through it to witness to the mighty deeds and love of God.

The Spirit's Gifts

In its working in and through the church the Spirit gives, nurtures, and coordinates certain gifts of praise and service. These gifts, whether rooted in natural talents and abilities or given miraculously through the power of the Spirit, are to be used for the upbuilding and edification of the whole community of faith; they are not to be a cause for boasting or division. Unfortunately, though, it seems that already in the early church, and particularly at Corinth, the gifts of the Spirit were used to divide rather than to unite its members in service (1 Cor. 1:10-31). Paul, on getting word of this, sends a stinging message to the congregation reminding them that they are all members of the one body of Christ and that their gifts are to be used for the edification of the church and its mission, not in competition and division. He makes it clear that the gifts of the Spirit are to be exercised in love and service within the church and in its outreach.

Specifically, Paul insists that the gift of tongues, speaking in inspired language, is to be used for the edification of the community, not for dividing it; and that this gift is to be exercised in praise and thanksgiving, not for boasting or exaltation over others. He acknowledges that prophecy is a gift from God, but he also insists that it too must be used in a way that unites and contributes to the whole community of faith in its mission, not for creating conflicts within the church. The New Testament writings give clear indication that prophecy has to be tested in the life and service of the church. The gift of healing implies openness to God's working in the whole of life, body and soul, to make life whole and well. The Spirit inspires some especially with this ministry, but the Spirit also works in the community as a whole to make it a healing community and a healing force in the world. Ministry, too, is a gift of the Spirit, and one that is to be exercised in a way that guides and equips all members of the church in their ministry.

In Galatians 5:22-26 Paul speaks of the "fruit of the Spirit" which is to be manifested in the lives of all believers. These qualities are to give evidence of their life in Christ; they are more than simply noble human traits, for they manifest the presence of Christ in the Christian individual and in the Christian community. Paul mentions specifically love, joy, peace, patience, kindness, goodness, faithfulness, gentleness, and self-control (Gal. 5:22-23). In other passages still other characteristics are added, such as forgiveness, putting away bitterness and malice, and holding fast to what is true and right (Eph. 4:30-32; Phil. 4:8).

In several texts it is suggested that the Holy Spirit is given to believers in and through the act of baptism (Acts 2:38; John 3:5); while some other texts suggest that the Spirit is given to the already baptized through the laying on of hands (which the church later formalized in rites of confirmation/chrismation; cf. Acts 8:14-17; 19:5-6). The Spirit here seems to be conveyed concretely to the believer, or its presence concretely symbolized or concentrated through these acts. These and other New Testament texts seem to indicate that the Spirit remains with the believer, empowering the person and community of faith in witness to Christ, especially in times of persecution (Mark 13:11-13). If this is true, then the church, guided and taught by the Spirit, cannot ultimately fail in witness to God's truth, although certainly there have been and are elements in its life that impede its witness to the truth and that render its witness too often as giving "mixed signals" to the world. For instance, its resignation to and complicity with forms of oppression cloud its proclamation of the God who exalts the lowly (Luke 1:52) and who in Christ has made us all sisters and brothers. The Spirit conveyed through baptism and confirmation/chrismation is a Spirit that works to break down and overcome all the barriers that separate us and stand in the way of our communion *(koinōnia)* in Christ.

We can sum this up by saying that all of the Spirit's gifts and graces are given so that the company of Christ's followers may manifest in its life more fully the living body of Christ, and thus become the sign and sacrament of God's will for the salvation of the world.

The Spirit, Christ, and the Church

The statements we have been making concerning the Spirit, Christ, and the church lead us to focus more sharply on the relation and connection of these three in the biblical drama. In the fabric of the biblical narrative each of these three has its distinctive identity; they do not simply merge with one another. At the same time neither are they separated from one another into air-tight compartments, as it were. Rather there seems to be an interrelation, even a mutual participation, among them that does not, however, obscure their integrity. Christ is the basis, "foundation" (1 Cor. 3:11), of the church (whether or not Jesus intentionally founded the church, a point debated by scholars). But the church is created, empowered, and sent forth in mission *post resurrectione Christi* in and by the Holy Spirit (see Acts 2 and 1 Cor. 12:3). The church as the community that believes and proclaims the gospel is the continuing living embodiment of Christ in the world through the grace of his presence in it (Matt. 18:20; Rom. 12:4) and the activity of the Spirit enabling its confession and life in Christ. But the church is also a struggling human community that always receives the presence of Christ and the Spirit by grace, and thus with gratitude and joy, and that prays and hopes that Christ and the Spirit will continue to be with it and will more fully inform its life (Rom. 8:26-27). Only so is the church a faithful witness in and to the movement of the Spirit.

But we must also say something more. For it is by the power of the Spirit, as we have seen, that Christ was anointed and commissioned in his ministry (Mark 1:10b-11), and it was by the power of the Spirit that he carried out his ministry of redemption. Thus, if it is this Spirit that comes from the Father through the Son who is at work in the life of the church, then the church is not merely a fortuitous consequence of God's redemption in Christ but is "organically" connected with that work (John 15:1-11), is in fact its extension or broadcasting, we might say, in and to the world. Thus, the Spirit extends through time and space the reality of Christ who is present concretely in the church as his body.

This involves both a tremendous source of strength and a high calling for the church. It means that the church is to follow its Lord in proclaiming the coming of God's new order in word and in deed. It means that the church is to show forth in its life the power of Christ's resurrection to sustain life against forces of destruction and death. It means too that the church must preach and teach with confidence and "authority," not simply because it claims to be authoritative but insofar as it "has the mind of Christ" and shows forth in its speech and action the Christ who himself does not so much claim authority as actually exercises it in ministry to those in need. When the church speaks and acts with such authority, it will be the first to recognize its weaknesses and constant need for ever deeper faith and faithfulness (see Matt. 8:26; 14:31; etc.). After the resurrection the Lord commissions the apostles, saying to them, not "I give you authority," but rather "full authority has been given to me. . . . Go therefore. . . ." Their mission is to manifest the Lord's authority, the authority of the servant, crucified Christ, who promises "I will be with you always, even to the end of time" (Matt. 28:20).

Among the apostles Peter had a special place (Matt. 16:13-20) and purpose, as Jesus indicates (Luke 22:32; John 21:15-19). He is the first apostle to profess who Jesus is (Matt. 16:13-16) and the first to preach the Good News (Acts 2:1-26). He is also led by the Spirit to a deeper and larger vision of God's mission through his encounter with Cornelius, a "God-fearing" centurion (Acts 10); and the text says his communication of this vision was accompanied by an outpouring of the Holy Spirit that confirmed what he was saying. His preaching of the gospel through the guidance of the Holy Spirit and in its power is what makes him the "rock" on which Christ builds the church. But it remains true that the chief cornerstone always was and will be Christ himself (Eph. 2:20; 1 Pet. 2:4-8).

The ministry entrusted to the apostles by the Lord continued after their deaths. Already during their lifetimes others, such as Paul, were drawn to share in their ministry of oversight and guidance of the flock which the Holy Spirit worked through them to shepherd (Acts 20:28). This ministry of oversight continues in the churches today. Some churches hold that this derives directly from the apostles through divine appointment, while other churches hold that it is a historically appropriate and beneficial ordering of the church, the "historic episcopate." Other churches believe that with the guidance of the Spirit the early Christian communities themselves designated leaders from among their members, and still other churches believe the Spirit acts in an extraordinary way to raise up and empower leaders/ministers of the church. Within the expanding early Christian community the offices of bishop, presbyter, and deacon emerged. Both ancient tradition and Scripture attest that persons were inducted into these offices by the laying on of hands and the invocation of the blessing and empowerment of the Holy Spirit (Acts 6:1-6; 13:2-3).

The continuing validity of this threefold office of ordained ministry is once more an issue before the churches. On the basis of recent biblical studies, the World Council of Churches in its Lima Document (more commonly known as BEM, standing for *Baptism, Eucharist and Ministry*)[9] has invited those churches who do not structure their ministry according to these offices to consider the values of adopting these offices for their own life and for the sake of the unity of the church. Also, the Consultation on Church Union (COCU), in its document calling for union in the Church of Christ Uniting,[10] proposes that the churches join in a covenanting partnership which recognizes the threefold ordained ministry. But even if agreement in practice can be reached among the churches on this matter, a basic theological question remains. It is the same question that has been much discussed between the Roman Catholic Church and the Eastern and Oriental Orthodox churches on the one hand, and between the Roman Catholic Church and those churches of the West that have the "historic episcopate," the Anglican, Lutheran, and Methodist churches, on the other. The question is, Is the threefold ministry, and particularly episcopacy, of the essence (the *esse*) of the church, or is it simply useful, a time-conditioned ordering (that is, of the *bene esse*) of the church? Underlying this issue is also, of course, the issue of the relationship of Scripture and tradition in the formation of the church.

9. *Baptism, Eucharist and Ministry,* Faith and Order Paper No. 111 (Geneva: World Council of Churches, 1982).

10. See Gerald F. Moede, ed., *The COCU Consensus: In Quest of a Church of Christ Uniting* (Princeton, NJ: Consultation on Church Union, 1985) and *Covenanting toward Unity: From Consensus to Communion* (Princeton, NJ: Consultation on Church Union, 1985), esp. 11ff.

The Activity of the Spirit in the Life of the Church

Certainly the activity of the Spirit in the life of the church is not limited only to its ordained ministry, although its oversight, direction, and sacramental and pastoral ministry are important means of the Spirit's action. As we see in the biblical narrative, the Holy Spirit is the bond of unity in the church (1 Cor. 12:13; Eph. 2:18; 4:4-6) and the source and power of its life (Rom. 8:2, 10; 2 Cor. 3:6). To confess that the Spirit is "the Lord and Giver of Life," in the words of the Nicene Creed, is to affirm not only the full divinity of the Spirit, who comes from the God who is "the fountain of life," but it is also to confess that the church which is filled with and which lives in the power of the Holy Spirit is itself sanctified and called to holiness. This holiness of dedication to God and being transformed by the power of God is to characterize all facets of the church's life. But nowhere is it to be more evident than in the church's worship. For here the community of faith is nourished, celebrates, and is renewed in Christ through the work of the Holy Spirit (John 4:23).

This is especially focused in the church's sacraments of baptism and the eucharist. The ancient churches of the East and of the West, which are sometimes referred to as "sacramental," hold that primarily in and through these acts the church is made holy, as are also individual believers. They view the seven sacraments as emerging as acts that communicate the grace of Christ to the community and nourish its life. They believe this happened from the impulse and under the guidance of the Holy Spirit. Those churches which practice only baptism (and confirmation/chrismation) and the Lord's Supper, or which do not practice any physical sacraments but observe what might be called a "sacramental" silence of spirituality, such as the Society of Friends (Quakers), experience through these acts concretely the presence of Christ and the power of the Spirit. Some churches testify to a second, special "baptism in/by the Holy Spirit" beyond water baptism. In these churches, too, the movement of the Holy Spirit is powerfully demonstrated.

All of these various forms and expressions of the Spirit have their roots in and are tested by the Pentecostal outpouring of the Spirit that inaugurated the church and that has formed and continues to inform and form its life. Nevertheless, issues remain as to how rightly to discern the Spirit in the life of the church and how to distinguish its activity and direction from the many other "spirits" of the world that manifest themselves also in the church. It is not surprising therefore that the question of how rightly to discern and follow the Spirit's leading becomes an issue of disagreement and even division in the life of the church. But the recognition that this is so should not become an excuse for resigning ourselves to such division, nor should it cause us to overlook that the Spirit can work even through these different perspectives to lead us to a fuller, deeper understanding of the Spirit. Here again we have to recognize that the church does not control the Spirit, but rather that the Spirit moves freely in and through the church. For instance, the Spirit elects Paul and Barnabas to preach to the Gentiles (Acts 13:2), even though this creates tension with the church in Jerusalem, and it is the Spirit that leads Paul and his companions from Asia Minor to Europe (Acts 16:6-10). Thus, while the Spirit dwells in and pervades the church, its movement in and through the church is dynamic and sometimes surprising; it nourishes the gifts of all its members, including those of our various church traditions — yet the Spirit works always to unite the community in holiness and love (Eph. 2:18).

The Holy Spirit and the Churches Today

A study of biblical themes and images concerning the Spirit helps us to discern more clearly the movement of the Spirit in the various branches of the Christian church today. As we have engaged in such study from the perspectives of our various church traditions, we have come to recognize and to appreciate more fully the work of the Spirit in these traditions. This has also helped us to discern more clearly the varied witness of Scripture to the Spirit. Furthermore, as we have attempted to discern the ongoing work of the Spirit in the life of the world, in the light of the scriptural witness, we have found that our various traditions provide important insights in this endeavor. And we have found that there are important understandings of the Spirit and its work in and through the church that we share. For instance, we are in agreement that the Spirit plays a key role in the inspiration, communication, and acceptance of sacred Scripture and its guidance for the church. The Spirit makes the Word of God vital and effective in the life of the church as well as in the lives of persons. This is a crucial matter of agreement among us, even though we still have differences over how precisely inspiration is to be understood — whether the Spirit inspires all the matters of which Scripture speaks or only those having to do centrally with saving faith — and how Scripture is to be interpreted in the church.

Another issue on which we find ourselves in essential and important agreement is that the Spirit is God's presence and power, nothing less, integral to the reality of God and at work in the church and in the world. We also agree that Scripture provides the basic guidelines for discerning the presence and work of the Spirit today, although there are some differences among us as to how more precisely these are to be applied and what they entail. The issue of how really to discern the Spirit, and how to distinguish God's Spirit from the many creaturely and even "false" spirits that manifest themselves among us is an issue with which we continue to struggle. For instance, how are we to recognize the Spirit in the remarkable events of our time? And how should we recognize the Spirit acting among us, especially within our church traditions and across church lines? In recent times much attention has been given in some church traditions to the "development of doctrine"; how should we discern the activity of the Spirit in this, and how distinguish its leading from the faddish currents of our times? Certainly not everything in our various church traditions equally manifests or is in line with the Spirit, but how should we "sort out" what is truly the work of the Spirit? And finally, as we struggle with our dividedness as churches, we cannot avoid the question: How can we continue to be divided when the Spirit which calls for and creates unity is at work among us?

What the Spirit seems to be saying to the churches today through Scripture is, "Share more fully in God's liberating and healing movement, 'with all humility and gentleness, with patience, bearing with one another through love, striving to preserve the unity of the spirit through the bond of peace'" (Eph. 4:2-3, The New American Bible).

Chapter Two

Discerning the Spirit in the Life of the Church

CECIL M. ROBECK, JR.

The Need for Discernment

A friend of mine sent a clipping to me from the San Francisco *Chronicle* recently. It was an article the *Chronicle*'s religion writer, Don Lattin, entitled "Two Faces of the Spiritual Revival." The subtitle announced, "New Agers and Pentecostals part of the same 'Great Awakening.'" Mr. Lattin chose his topic after Phillip Lucas of the University of California at Santa Barbara presented a paper on this subject at the 1989 meeting of the American Academy of Religion in Anaheim, California.

Based upon Lucas's research, Lattin reported a number of striking similarities between the two movements:

1. "Both seek guidance from spirits and a direct experience of the sacred. . . .

Cecil M. Robeck, Jr., an ordained minister of the Assemblies of God, serves as associate professor of church history and ecumenics at Fuller Theological Seminary in Pasadena, California. His ecumenical activities include membership on the Plenary Commission on Faith and Order of the WCC and co-chair of the International Roman Catholic-Pentecostal Dialogue. He served as editor of *Pneuma: The Journal of the Society for Pentecostal Studies,* from 1984-1992 and is author of the recent volume *Prophecy in Carthage: Perpetua, Tertullian, and Cyprian* (Cleveland: Pilgrim Press, 1992).

2. "Both see the world on the edge of a radical spiritual transformation, whether it is called the 'New Age' or the 'Millennium.'

3. "Both stress spiritual and physical healing through the laying on of hands, prayer, crystals or other techniques outside medical science.

4. "Both arose as movements outside the mainline churches but have grown to the extent they are now subtly changing the beliefs and worship styles of the religious establishment."[1]

Mr. Lattin went on in his newspaper account to cite several other similarities, but these are sufficient to set the stage for the discussion at hand.

On the surface, it is difficult to deny that the similarities to which Lucas pointed exist. They do. At least they do on a phenomenological level. But when probed more deeply, the differences between these two movements more than offset the similarities described in the article. Pentecostals distinguish themselves from the New Age movement by pointing to affinities between much New Age teaching and that of certain Eastern religions, especially Hinduism. On the other hand, many New Agers look down upon Pentecostals as nothing more than pulpit-pounding, Bible-thumping Fundamentalists with a supernatural twist.

Newspaper writer Don Lattin questioned Pentecostal pastor David Cawston about the New Age movement and received the following comment: "Our [Pentecostal's] one authority is the Bible, and the Bible tells us that every spirit is not of Christ. . . . There are many spirits in the world, and some of them are very deceptive."[2] Cawston went on to note that the spirit which he saw in the New Age Movement was not the Holy Spirit. New Age was not, therefore, a legitimate manifestation of the church.

But when reporter Lattin talked with Michael Anast, head of the New Age's Foundation for Spiritual Freedom, Mr. Anast denied that the New Age movement was "doing anything outside what the Bible

---

1. Don Lattin, "Two Faces of the Spiritual Revival," *San Francisco Chronicle,* 1 Dec. 1989, sec. B3. I owe my awareness of this article to Mr. Tom Pratt. Much of the introduction was published previously in the editorial, "Discernment: Insight into the Mind of Christ," in *Pneuma: The Journal of the Society for Pentecostal Studies* 11:2 (Fall 1989), 73-76. It is used here by permission.

2. Ibid., 6.

says."[3] In short, he argued that if it did not hold a legitimate place within the church, he wanted it understood that the teachings of the New Age movement were at least not inconsistent with the church's teaching.

This essay confronts us with a classic question. How do we discern what is within and what is outside of the church when we meet a movement, denomination, or even a congregation that claims to be inspired by the Spirit? How does the church know in such instances whether or not it is dealing with another part of the church, or with something else? Jesus warned his own disciples that there would be those who would come into their midst as wolves in sheep's clothing (Matt. 7:15-23), intent upon leading even the elect astray (Matt. 24:11, 24-25; Mark 13:22-23). They might take to themselves the *appearance* of being legitimate members of the church, but they would not *be* legitimate members of the church. What makes it possible for Christians to recognize each other as Christians, and movements and denominations to recognize each other as being legitimate parts of the universal church? Is it a certain form? Is it a certain content? Is it certain words? Or certain actions? Or is it something else? To what authority do Christians appeal when making such judgments? Scripture? Tradition? Reason? Experience? Praxis? Or is it some combination of these factors to which they appeal? And what role does the Spirit play in this?

David Cawston, the Pentecostal pastor, saw his own tradition standing within the stream of historic biblical Christianity. Scripture is its ultimate authority, he argued. But when the Pentecostal movement first appeared on the religious landscape at the beginning of this century, it was denounced from pulpits as religion which preached a "rank counterfeit."[4] It was caricatured as "a disgusting amalgamation of African voodoo superstition and Caucasian insanity."[5] The president of the Los Angeles Church Federation, troubled by the emergence of Pentecostalism in 1906, described it as embodying "enthusiastic fanaticism"[6] and warned that some of the enthusiasts "might lose their reason through over zeal and become dangerous."[7] Indeed, many were arrested and hospitalized on charges of insanity.[8] Pentecostals

---

3. Ibid.
4. "Local Knights Go to Pomona," *Los Angeles Herald*, 21 July 1906, p. 7.
5. "New Religions Come, Then Go," *Los Angeles Herald*, 24 Sept. 1906, p. 7.
6. "Churches Aroused to Action," *Los Angeles Express*, 18 July 1906, p. 1.
7. "Young Girl Given Gift of Tongues," *Los Angeles Express*, 20 July 1906, p. 1.

were derogatorily labeled "Holy Jumpers," "Holy Kickers," "Holy Rollers," "Tangled Tonguers," and the "Tongues Movement." While Pentecostals would hardly be considered by many Christians as occupying *the* centrist position within the church, from many quarters in the church they are now viewed as a legitimate and vibrant part of the church, even by many who once rejected their claims to legitimacy.[9] How did this change come about? The answer, in part, may lie in a charism of the Holy Spirit graciously given to the church, the ability to distinguish between spirits.

The Discernment of Spirits in Scripture

Within the New Testament the concept of discernment is explicitly linked to the Holy Spirit through Paul's claim that the Spirit grants "the ability to distinguish between spirits" (1 Cor. 12:10-11).[10] This gift or charism appears adjacent to the gift of prophecy within the classic Pauline catalogue of charisms. Its connection with the gift of prophecy in 1 Corinthians 14:29 suggests that it is important for us to think of these two gifts as "paired" gifts in much the same way that the charism of "speaking in tongues" is paired with "the interpretation of tongues" (1 Cor. 12:10; 14:4-5, 13, 27-28). The exercise of the prophetic gift anticipates the exercise of the discerning gift.[11] Those who discern, who weigh or test what is said prophetically, provide a significant service to the Christian community.

8. " 'Holy Roller' Mad," *Los Angeles Daily Times,* 18 July 1906, sec. II, p. 17; "An Insane 'Roller,' " *Los Angeles Daily Times,* 10 Sept. 1906, p. 18; "Fanatics Cause Loss of Mind," *Los Angeles Record,* 10 Sept. 1906, p. 5.

9. Harold B. Smith, ed., *Pentecostals from the Inside Out* (Wheaton: Victor Books, 1990), 9.

10. The most significant treatments of discernment of spirits to date include Casiano Floristan and Christian Duquoc, *Discernment of the Spirit and of Spirits,* Concilium 119 (New York: Seabury Press/Crossroad, 1979); Jacques Guillet et al., *Discernment of Spirits,* trans. Innocentia Richards (Collegeville, MN: Liturgical Press, 1970); Thomas Dubay, S.M., *Authenticity: A Biblical Theology of Discernment* (Denville, NJ: Dimension Books, 1977); and Morton Kelsey, *Discernment: A Study in Ecstasy and Evil* (New York: Paulist Press, 1978).

11. James D. G. Dunn, "Discernment of Spirits — A Neglected Gift," in *Witness to the Spirit: Essays on Revelation, Spirit, Redemption,* ed. W. Harrington (Dublin: Irish Biblical Association, 1979), 80. Dunn notes the linkage between these gifts in Paul's writings as well as the tendency in the modern church to separate them.

Two terms in the New Testament describe the process of discernment. The first, used by Paul in 1 Corinthians 12:10, is *diakriseis pneumatōn*. That the term *discernment* does not appear alone is significant. It is the discernment *of spirits*. Most scholars suggest that the discernment to which Paul refers here is discernment of the *source* of prophetic claims. What spirit inspires the prophetic utterance? Is it the Holy Spirit, the Spirit of God, or is it some other spirit? But the assessment of prophetic *content* is also not totally absent, since this is clearly in mind in Paul's use of the term in 1 Corinthians 14:29. Following any prophetic utterance, he says others are to "weigh *(diakrinetōsan)* what is said."

A second verb which bears upon this discussion is *dokimazō*. It, too, is employed by Paul, but it appears mainly in his exhortation to the Thessalonian congregation. As in 1 Corinthians, this verb stands in relationship to the prophetic gift. "Do not quench the Spirit," writes Paul, "do not despise prophesying, but test *(dokimazete)* everything; hold fast what is good, abstain from every form of evil" (1 Thess. 5:19-22). In this text, the emphasis is clearly upon prophetic *content*. Similarly, in 1 John 4:1-6 this verb is employed in a manner consistent with the Pauline position. John's readers are exhorted to "test the spirits *(dokimazete ta pneumata)* to see whether they are of God. . . ." In this case, the discernment is applied once again to prophetic claims and specifically to the central claim of the humanity of Jesus Christ. Those who do not confess Jesus Christ as come in the flesh are judged as being "not of God."

Pastor Cawston's opinion of the New Age movement includes a concern for the discernment of spirits. He assumes that Pentecostals are in fellowship with the Holy Spirit who speaks through Scripture. Scripture, in turn, acts as the ultimate norm for Christian faith and life. New Age claims, he suggests, may well be dependent upon some other spirit or spirits for their inspiration. In raising this concern, he stands within the long tradition of the people of God. Jeremiah warned the people of Israel to ignore the cultic prophets of his own day who spoke "visions of their own minds" (Jer. 23:16). Likewise, the Deuteronomist warned Israel to be alert to those who, in prophetic guise, "prophesied" things which, if followed, would move them away from God (Deut. 13:1-3).[12]

12. For a brief discussion of testing prophetic claims, see Cecil M. Robeck, Jr.,

In the midst of the jumble of everyday life, discernment of spirits is not always easily accomplished. There were those in Israel who believed the words of the cultic prophets even when their messages were not from God. History is full of illustrations of those who followed false prophets, false teachers, and false messiahs (cf. Mark 13:22). One need think only as far as the Jonestown tragedy in our own day to observe the horrible outcome of not discerning between true and false religious claims.[13]

While discernment may be associated in the biblical tradition most specifically with prophetic words and inspiring "spirits," the expansion of the concept and the development of the practice of a more broadly defined "discernment" is clearly consistent with the narrower description given by Paul's phrase, the discerning of spirits. Repeatedly the people of God are confronted with ethical, moral, and doctrinal choices. In Deuteronomy 30:19 the choice is between life and blessing, or death and being cursed. In Psalm 1:6 there is a righteous way of life known by Yahweh, or the way of the wicked marked by death. Jeremiah 21:8 observes that the way of life is the way of surrender, while the way of death is typified by resistance.[14] Proper choices in faith and life require discernment, broadly conceived; and discernment necessarily contains an ethical dimension.

Discernment is accomplished in reliance upon God through the work of God's Spirit. It is to be undertaken within the context of the *koinōnia* as a gift which serves the needs of the entire body of Christ (1 Cor. 12:7). Like all gifts, its use is to be accomplished in love (1 Cor. 13:1–14:1), not as a means to gain personal or institutional

---

"Prophetic Authority in the Charismatic Setting: The Need to Test," *Theological Renewal* 24 (July 1983): 4-10. For an extended discussion of continuing prophecy in the period of the developing canon, see Cecil M. Robeck, Jr., "Canon, *Regulae Fidei*, and Continuing Revelation in the Early Church," in *Church, Word, and Spirit* ed. James E. Bradley and Richard A. Muller (Grand Rapids, MI: Eerdmans, 1987), 65-91.

13. Jim Jones was originally an independent Pentecostal minister while serving as pastor of People's Temple in Indianapolis during the mid-1950s. Three of his sermons from this period are "Leaving the Church," *Herald of Faith* 22:3, March 1956, 15; "As a Man Thinketh So He Is," *Herald of Faith* 22:5, May 1956, 8, 10-11; "Faith Without Works Is Dead," *Herald of Faith* 22:12, Dec. 1956, 11, 21.

14. Qumran's *Manual of Discipline* describes a division between the way of light and the way of darkness (1QS 3:13–4:26). *The Testament of Asher* 3:1-2 sets forth two ways of life. Cf. *4 Ezra* 7:6-8; Matt. 7:14; Heb. 5:14; *Didache* 1:1; *Epistle of Barnabas* 18–20.

power. Scripture provides a number of tests whereby discernment may be accomplished. Many of these tests incorporate criteria which are based upon common sense, shared community values, or a set of doctrinal standards. In our life together the church is called repeatedly to engage in the process of discernment. To help us find useful criteria which may enlighten the church and enable it more effectively to discern the claims of newer religious movements, a brief survey of how discernment occurs within the biblical tradition may be useful.

Discerning Claims of Inspiration

Kenneth Hagin has said:

> For years I have travelled extensively in the ministry. Everywhere I go there is always somebody who has a "word" from the Lord for me — sometimes two or three. In all these years only one or two of them have been correct.[15]

Modern Pentecostalism, and the broader charismatic renewal, confronts us with the need for discernment in much the same way that the early church was confronted with this need. Independent charismatic evangelist Kenneth Hagin, no stranger to prophetic claims himself, is nevertheless openly critical of and concerned about the lack of judgment given to many truth claims, and even to many prophetic claims today. Issues of authority, of power, of leadership, and of truth present themselves immediately when someone or some group presumes to speak on behalf of God. Messenger formulas such as "Thus saith the Lord," or "The Lord told me to tell you" can be incredibly intimidating to those who are confronted by them. The words which follow these formulas require serious consideration. But precisely because these phrases are so powerful, some who would claim prophetic status use them to their own advantage. In all too many cases the phrase may mean nothing more than "I think that . . ." or "I want you to. . . ." It is therefore important to realize that such claims to divine inspiration call for immediate analysis, and the limited but useful guidelines available in Scripture and developed within the context of

15. Kenneth Hagin, *How You Can Be Led by the Spirit of God* (Tulsa: Kenneth Hagin Ministries, 1979), 108.

the people of God are still relevant. Chief among these criteria are the following:

1. Who or What Is the Source of Inspiration?

The Pauline corpus employs a number of metaphors to describe the church. One of the most frequently used is the metaphor which depicts the church as the body of Christ (1 Cor. 12:12-28; Rom. 12:3-8; Eph. 4:4-16). In each of the passages in which it appears, this powerful metaphor provides a context in which the subject of charisms is also addressed. Issues such as the relationship between members of the whole church (diversity) and the relationship of each and of all members to the one church (unity) quickly surface in the discussion as well.

Of importance to us is the realization that within the church God has raised up individuals to minister and to accomplish the work toward which God directs them. Some are concerned with the internal working of the body (such as pastors or teachers). Others are concerned with reaching out into the community (e.g., evangelists, those who give aid or do acts of mercy, etc.). Still others hold the potential to enable the church to worship God in profound and mysterious ways (speakers in tongues and interpreters of tongues, etc.), or become mouthpieces for God to the church or the world (prophets, exhorters, those with words of wisdom or knowledge, etc.). In each case the charism or gift is given at the sovereign will of God (1 Cor. 12:11) as a manifestation of God's varied grace (1 Cor. 12:4-7; Rom. 12:6; Eph. 4:7; 1 Pet. 4:10-11). It is given for the common good (1 Cor. 12:7). God's Spirit, then, is at work in the church and in the life of believers who, indwelt by the Spirit (Rom. 8:9; 1 Cor. 12:12-13, 27), make up the church.

But inspiration per se is not limited only to the church. Neither is it, in the words of James D. G. Dunn, "self-authenticating."[16] Luke notes that when Paul and Silas were in Philippi they were confronted daily by a young woman who followed them as they went toward their place of prayer. "These men are servants of the Most High God who proclaim to you the way of salvation" (Acts 16:17), she announced. But Luke notes that she had a "spirit of divination *(pneuma pythōna)*" by which she was inspired to tell fortunes for a fee. Paul was deeply troubled by this woman's plight, and he exorcised the spirit of divi-

---

16. Dunn, "Discernment of Spirits — A Neglected Gift," 80.

nation. A spirit other than the Spirit of God was responsible for her "inspired" actions.

The ancient world believed in many alternative sources of inspiration. Throughout Mesopotamia, in the Mari letters, and among the Assyrians, both prior to and concurrent with Israel's prophetic claims, there were others who saw their inspiration as coming not from Yahweh, but from one or another god or spirit.[17] Some of these were understood by Israel to be forms of divination (Deut. 18:10-11) and were expressly forbidden among the people of God. Within the Greek and Roman worlds there were many prophetic claims, especially surrounding Zeus at Dodona and Apollo at Delphi.[18] Early Christians who were confronted by these claims consistently condemned them as demonically inspired.[19] The church was continually called upon to assess the legitimacy of such claims by discerning the source of their inspiration.

The knowledge that not all claims of inspiration can be accepted at face value is an important step in discerning true from false claims. Claims of authority based upon spirits other than God's Spirit can safely be ignored. The determination of the source of a prophetic word or a truth claim is, therefore, critical. But there are other criteria which can be employed in discernment as well. One such criterion is related to the *form* in which the alleged inspiration is manifested.

2. How Do Those Who Are Inspired Act?

Jesus warned his disciples that false prophets, those who parade as wolves in sheep's clothing, would ultimately be discerned through the fruit they produce (Matt. 7:16-18). The production of good fruit suggests a good tree as its source, while evil fruit indicates a bad one. There is a relationship between what is produced, that is, what may ultimately be observed, and the genuineness or authenticity of the one who produces it. There is also a relationship between what is produced and the way one goes about producing. In each case there is an ethical dimension which is essential to the discerning process. The Christian character of those involved becomes part of the mix.

17. Robert R. Wilson, *Prophecy and Society in Ancient Israel* (Philadelphia: Fortress Press, 1980), esp. 89-134.

18. Plutarch, *Obsolescence of Oracles* 414B, E.

19. Justin Martyr, *Apology* 1.18, 44, 56; Origen, *Against Celsus* 7.7.3-4; Tertullian, *Apology* 1.22.

In 1 Corinthians 14:33, Paul states that "God is not a God of confusion but of peace." He argues that the exercise of the charisms should be consistent with the character of the one who gives them. Hence, the proper exercise of these gifts, the way these charisms are to be used, is "decently and in order" (1 Cor. 14:39). They are to result in such things as "upbuilding and encouragement and consolation" (1 Cor. 14:3-5, 26, 31). If the ultimate fruit of any prophetic claim is destruction, contradiction, confusion, disruption, and chaos, Paul suggests, then the one who makes the prophetic claim is not doing so in the power of God's Spirit. Paul's emphasis upon good fruit in every aspect of one's life is important to note (Gal. 5:18, 22, 25), just as is the repudiation of all works of the flesh (Gal. 5:19-21).

In spite of this, since gifts come as a manifestation of grace, they often come in fresh ways in the mature and the immature alike. They come irrespective of personal claims of sanctification or of piety. Yet they come within the context of fellowship *(koinōnia)* and are to be given and received in love, in a decent and orderly fashion. But contexts may vary, and what is decent and in order may vary to some extent in different contexts. For instance, decent and orderly behavior at a sporting event differs markedly from decent and orderly behavior in a classroom; but that does not mean that one is right and the other wrong. The context must determine that. Paul implies in his letter to Corinth that when everyone in the congregation understands and is able fully to participate in the assembly, what constitutes decency and orderliness differs from that standard of decency and orderliness which is expected when an unbeliever or an outsider enters (1 Cor. 14:13-17, 23-25). But this, too, is related to the fruit which is produced. Jesus announced that the Paraclete whom God would send would be in and with us (John 14:17), would teach and remind us (John 14:26), would convince the world of "sin, righteousness, and judgment" (John 16:8-10), would guide us into all truth by revealing the mind of God to us (John 16:13-14), and perhaps most importantly, the Paraclete would bear witness to Jesus (John 15:26) and glorify him (John 16:14).

There is a strong suggestion of trinitarian theology here. But there is an even stronger implication that those who claim the presence of the Spirit in their lives and midst can be expected to manifest fruit which is consistent with the Spirit's presence. One might expect that there would be alternative forms of this fruit, in that the work of the Spirit is likened to the wind — unpredictable, perhaps serendipitous in its movement. Nonetheless, manifested in these works in all their variety is the Holy Spirit (John 3:8). Legitimate prophetic claims might be manifest within or at times apart from traditional ecclesiastical structures. But those who would call attention to themselves in such a way as to detract from the centrality, the uniqueness, or the importance of Jesus Christ, whether through arrogance, triumphalism, deceit, or confusion, clearly do not bear the fruit of the presence of the Spirit whom they claim to possess.

Furthermore, an unwillingness to cooperate in the discernment process is itself an indication that something is wrong. Those who claim inspiration must be open to assessment, review, and critique. Jesus assumed this in his admonition that the false claimant would be known by the fruit produced. John commanded it in his exhortation to "test the spirits to see whether they are of God" (1 John 4:1), and went on to suggest that only those who followed his command were truly listening to and obeying God (1 John 4:6). Paul exhorted the Thessalonians to test everything, to sort through the good and evil, and to hold fast to the good (1 Thess. 5:21-22). He even claimed divine support when he told the Corinthians that what he had stated was a "command of the Lord" whose authority was the ultimate key to their recognition (1 Cor. 14:37-38). Those who refused to submit to the testing process were not to be given credence.

3. What Is Said through Inspiration?

A third criterion in the discernment of the Spirit has to do with the analysis of content. In order to assess whether the content is truly of the Spirit, it must be judged against some standard or norm. Within the larger Christian context of the twentieth century the standard is normally understood to be the canon of Scripture. Tradition, the formulation of *regulae fidei*, creeds, or rules of faith which are believed to be consistent with and/or derived from the "apostolic faith" as it has been delivered in Scripture, as well as definitions of apostolicity, reason, and experience, may be viewed as playing secondary roles here. The extent to which particular claims are consistent with, complement, compete with, contradict, or supersede these criteria, especially the canon of Scripture, helps us determine whether they are legitimate or not legitimate, and thus of the Spirit.

Yet, if the Spirit's work is as unpredictable as the wind, then those who expect to discern the presence of the Spirit must be open to the unpredictable, to the new and to the spontaneous. There are limits to this unpredictability, however, and these limits are important to the discerning process. The writer to the Hebrews reports that God has spoken in a variety of ways through an array of people, but in these last days God has spoken through Jesus Christ (Heb. 1:1-2). Thus, Jesus' own life and teachings must be seen as normative. Those who seek to undermine what is said by God through Christ are not to be accepted. In John's day, it was those who denied the full humanity of Jesus (1 John 4:2-3). Paul was concerned about those who might claim inspiration yet "curse" Jesus (1 Cor. 12:3); and in Ephesians 4:11-16 it is obvious that some gifts were given to the church to protect it from those who might advocate "every wind of doctrine," or resort to deceiving the church by the use of "human cunning" and "deceitful wiles." In each case, the words or teachings of those who are to be disregarded provide clues to their ultimate source of inspiration.

Words are sometimes confusing, however, and are open to and in need of interpretation. Sometimes the immediate context helps. At other times it is necessary to rely upon additional knowledge. One word attributed to the New Testament prophet Agabus provides a concrete example of this. Acts 21 describes a portion of Paul's third missionary trip. Paul stopped in Caesarea to spend several days with Philip the evangelist and his four prophesying daughters. Agabus met them there. Taking Paul's girdle, he bound his own feet and hands in a symbolic action and said, "Thus says the Holy Spirit." The oracle which followed stated simply, "So shall the Jews at Jerusalem bind the man who owns this girdle and deliver him into the hands of the Gentiles" (Acts 21:11).

Within the context of that meeting the various parties disagreed as to what the utterance meant and how Paul should respond to it. The majority heard the prediction and interpreted it as having the meaning of a *warning*. Paul, they argued, should not go to Jerusalem. That is what the Spirit was saying. The apostle, however, did not share this majority opinion. His own experience suggested that he was "bound in the Spirit" (Acts 20:22) to go to Jerusalem. Along his journey he had heard several predictions that he would be imprisoned when he arrived in Jerusalem (Acts 20:22-23). Others had already suggested that the Spirit was telling him not to go on (Acts 21:4).

Still, Paul did not view the utterance as a directive of the Spirit not to go but merely as *predictive* of what he might encounter there. Paul would not go back. He would go on, bound in the Spirit, and he would suffer for his faith.

The result was that when Agabus appeared before Paul at Caesarea and the others "weighed" what Agabus said, Paul still prevailed. His assessment was based upon prior knowledge rooted in revelation by the Spirit, or upon an experience of the Spirit by which he was "bound" to continue his journey. Ultimately, they sent him on to Jerusalem with a prayer that "the will of the Lord be done" (Acts 21:14). The ultimate test of the veracity of Agabus as a prophet would be the test of fulfillment, an ancient test (Deut. 18:22). It was a test which Agabus had already passed on one occasion a decade or so earlier (Acts 11:28). But if this were a predictive word, it needed to be weighed and tested on its own merits.

If claims are open to interpretation, then there needs to be some flexibility built into the objective testing of the spiritual basis of such claims. The correct interpretation may not always be instantly clear. Something more may be necessary in the discernment process. In spite of this, the assessment of prophetic claims by analyzing the words spoken or teachings projected under the claim of inspired speech is a helpful criterion in discerning whether such claims are truly of the Spirit. Those claims that counter the direct and clear teaching of the Christian canon, Scripture, may safely be ignored.

There are also those who claim to have supplemental revelation. In our own day we have witnessed Mormon claims which suggest that, in addition to Scripture, other "inspired" or "revealed" works play an important if not canonical role of one sort or other.[20] In the patristic

---

20. *The Book of Mormon, The Pearl of Great Price,* and *The Doctrine and Covenant of the Church of Jesus Christ of Latter Day Saints* are all examples of this in the LDS tradition. D. S. Crowther's *Gifts of the Spirit* (Bountiful, UT: Horizon, 1983) provides an extended discussion on the topic. In the Seventh Day Adventist tradition one may study A. G. Daniells, *The Abiding Light of Prophecy* (Mountain View, CA: Pacific Press, 1936); W. A. Spicer, *The Spirit of Prophecy in the Adventist Movement: A Gift That Builds Up* (Washington, D.C.: Review and Herald, 1936). It might also be suggested that a parallel to *ex cathedra* statements by the Pope in Roman Catholic doctrine might also be seen here. Pentecostals and charismatics are sometimes criticized for accepting, even with limitations, *any* contemporary prophetic claim as a word from God. See Walter Chantry, *Signs of the Apostles: Obervations on Pentecostalism Old and New* (Edinburgh: Banner of Truth Trust, 1975, rev. 1976), 22-27.

era, Montanists in Asia Minor and in North Africa moved beyond the boundaries of the commonly used Scriptures and appealed to other allegedly inspired visions and revelations. Furthermore, certain Gnostics reveled in the idea that their contemporary revelations superseded the apostolic ones.[21]

Contemporary scholarship does not typically treat the Montanists as heretics, nor does it criticize Montanist teaching as harshly as in earlier days. Current criticism typically takes into consideration a number of sociological factors that pertain to that development, including questions of the relationship between the authority of Montanist prophetic claims and the competing claims to authority made by the early bishops. Criticism is also made of the actions which the Montanists mandated as a result of their "revelations." This parallels the judgment of many early Christians. The Montanists of Tertullian's day were put on the defensive as charged with inventing "novel" and "burdensome" disciplines.[22] Jerome criticized the Montanists for embracing prophets whose utterances failed "to accord with the Scriptures old and new," and he chided them for making certain traditions obligatory which he believed should be matters of choice.[23] Tertullian himself labored under such charges, arguing that contemporary appeal to the Paraclete was an appeal to the Spirit as "restitutor" rather than as "institutor."[24] But extreme care must be taken to test all claims of inspiration, especially those made apart from the Judeo-Christian tradition and those which claim authoritative status in the lives of the faithful.

4. How Do We Experience the Spirit?

Whenever we speak of the spiritual realm we have difficulty trying to grasp what it is all about. That it exists, we would not deny, but it stretches us to try to understand it conceptually. This is also true of the role which personality plays in the exercise of the charisms. That

---

21. Irenaeus, *Against Heresies* 1.13.6; 1.25.2; 3.12.12; Tertullian, *Prescription Against Heretics* 23.1; Zostrianus (CG 8.1.14). Other examples are cited in Pheme Perkins, *The Gnostic Dialogue: The Early Church and the Crisis of Gnosticism* (New York: Paulist Press, 1980), 81.

22. Tertullian, *On Monogamy* 2.2.

23. Jerome, *Epistle* 41.2.3; cf. Tertullian, *On Fasting* 2.1-4.

24. Tertullian, *On Monogamy* 4.1.

it plays a part is clear, but where the distinction lies between the grace of God in the impartation of gifts by God's Spirit, and the grace of God as it is manifest in the "natural" realm of the human psyche and our natural talents and abilities is difficult to assess. Yet in the discerning of spirits it is important to distinguish and understand the role which God plays, the role which we play, and the role which any other spirit might play.

Paul understood that there was a legitimate role for experience in the exercise of the charisms. Some Corinthians were satisfied to speak in tongues within the public assembly, and to leave their utterances uninterpreted, unexplained, and unchallenged. Paul disagreed. This practice did not edify the others who were present (1 Cor. 14:16-19), and it held the potential that might cause the unbelieving visitor to miss completely the presence of God (1 Cor. 14:23). Paul believed that speaking in tongues was a form of trans-rational or pre-conceptual prayer.[25] "If I pray in a tongue," Paul argued, "my Spirit prays *(to pneuma mou proseuchetai)* but my mind is unfruitful *(nous mou akarpos estin)*" (1 Cor. 14:14). While scholars have debated the significance of the phrase "my spirit," in light of Paul's assertion that "speaking in tongues" is a charism given by God's Spirit, the phrase "my spirit" must necessarily take cognizance of Paul's assertion. The Holy Spirit, speaking through the Christian, in some way enters into the experience of the Christian, but at the same time the Spirit may bypass the rational or conceptual processes of human personality (Rom. 8:26-27).

Something similar must be said of the Spirit's role in the discerning of spirits. Paul notes that it is the Spirit who bears "witness with our spirit that we are children of God" (Rom. 8:16). While rationality may play a role here, the role of intuition, of trans-rationality, or the *experience* of assurance is not absent. Indeed, the experience of some suggests that the ability to discern with the aid of the Spirit of God may involve a flash of insight, a sudden impulse of recognition, or a divine revelation even independent of rationality or conceptual processes. It may be a deep-seated sense or feeling which validates the claim.

Paul contends that to those who have the Spirit (Rom. 8:9), the

25. For a discussion of "pre-conceptual prayer," see George T. Montague, S.M., *The Spirit and His Gifts* (New York: Paulist Press, 1974), 21.

Spirit bears witness *(symmartyrei)* that they are the children of God (Rom. 8:16). That Spirit provides a confirmation of relationship, a testimony of assonance or of assurance between God and the children of God. It is only a small step in logic, then, to posit that the discernment of the Spirit is merely a recognition or illumination, or an inner testimony that others, too, have the same Spirit and are therefore children of God, or that they do not have the Spirit and therefore are not children of God.

The role of *koinōnia* is central to this. The Spirit in whom the church participates (Phil. 2:1), and through whom *koinōnia* is experienced (2 Cor. 13:13 [14]) is the same Spirit who enables those who have the Spirit to affirm their relationship to God. But as John points out, *koinōnia* is not fully understood or experienced without recognizing that it defines the relationship of the individual to God, the relationships among all those who experience or have the Spirit, and the relationship between God and all who have the Spirit (1 John 1:3, 6-7).

Peter's confession that Jesus was "the Christ, the Son of the living God" came to him by means of divine revelation (Matt. 16:16-17), which was clearly a work of God's Spirit (John 15:26). That revelation need not have come by words, but as a flash of insight, a deeply rooted sense of continuity with Israel's prophetic past and present, or as an internal witness that affected Peter's spiritual sensitivity. Similarly, Jesus' spontaneously unrehearsed conversation with the woman at the well enabled her to move from her initial impression that he was an unusual Jewish man (John 3:9), to her recognition of him as a prophet (John 3:19), to her ultimate embrace of Jesus as the Christ (John 3:29, 39). And in the post-apostolic period, Hermas contended that false prophets could be discerned when the righteous who possessed the Spirit *(pneuma theotetos)* prayed together.[26]

In arguing for a role for feeling, for the senses, and for experience in the discernment of the Spirit, it must be noted that not everything which provides a sense of spiritual well-being is necessarily from the Holy Spirit. A recent "Letter to the Bishops of the Catholic Church," issued by Cardinal Joseph Ratzinger on behalf of the Doctrinal Congregation under the title "Some Aspects of Christian Meditation," warns the bishops that there is a tendency for some Christians to rely

---

26. Hermas, *Mandate* 11.14.

too heavily upon feelings engendered by certain meditative practices which are modeled on practices characteristic of Hinduism and Buddhism, such as those found in Zen, Transcendental Meditation, and Yoga. The document notes:

> Some physical exercises automatically produce a feeling of quiet and relaxation, pleasing sensations, perhaps even phenomena of light and of warmth, which resemble spiritual well-being. To take such feelings for the authentic consolations of the Holy Spirit would be a totally erroneous way of conceiving the spiritual life.[27]

Feelings alone, even warm and nurturing feelings, are not necessarily trustworthy manifestations of the Spirit. Nor do they always enable those who experience them to understand their meaning or source.

Discerning the Church through the Spirit

Our discussion thus far has focused upon a need which the church must take seriously in an increasingly secularized and pluralistic age. It is the need for greater spiritual discernment. In our review of the subject, we have looked carefully at some of the biblical criteria which contribute to an understanding of the gift of the discerning of spirits and how these function. We are now in a position to apply some of these principles more broadly so as to enable us better to discern the presence of the church by the Spirit.[28]

It is surely the case that the Spirit of God is present throughout the created order. The *ruach Yahweh* was present in the primal chaos, "brooding," as it were, over creation (Gen. 1:1-2). The Spirit continues to play an active role in human existence (John 16:7-11). Indeed, the Spirit *may* speak at times even through those who do not profess Christ, such as a Mahatma Gandhi. Within the context of the church, however, the Spirit is never separated from the One who sends the Spirit, nor from the Christ to whom the Spirit bears witness (John

---

27. "Some Aspects of Christian Meditation," *Origins*, 19:30, Dec. 1989, 496.

28. To advocate an expansion of the idea of discernment at this point is not to advocate an individualized form of discernment. Discernment is first and foremost a function of the Spirit in the church and should be understood as best expressed in a community process.

16:13-15). Of significance in the discerning process, then, is the question of what role the christological affirmation plays.

The confession "Jesus is Lord" was critical to early Christian life.[29] And it remains critical in the life of church, not merely as a creedal affirmation but also as a guide to a second concern, namely, the shaping of the life of the church. Christian life involves submission to the Lordship of Christ. Central to this is the issue of ethics. Pentecostal preaching has traditionally made a plea for personal ethics, with the expectation that social and institutional ethics would necessarily fall into line with transformed lives. The work of the Holy Spirit in transforming, or, as some would say, in sanctifying the life of the church, whether this comes through the mortification of the flesh (Rom. 8:13) or the growth of spiritual fruit (Gal. 5:22-25), is a critical role of the Spirit who is Holy in shaping the Christian life. The earliest church took this role seriously and looked for clues which would point toward authentic ministry. The writer of the *Didache* discerned the presence of the Spirit in the ministry of prophets by the willingness of the prophet to take on certain limitations, to speak on behalf of others without concern for his or her own personal welfare. The church, too, in response to the Spirit's presence, must be ready to demonstrate self-limitation under the Lordship of Christ.

Even though the presence of the Holy Spirit enables the church to discern itself, discernment remains a difficult task. This should come as no surprise. In the midst of his discussion on the charisms in 1 Corinthians 12–14, Paul candidly observed that during the present age, "we see in a mirror dimly . . ." (1 Cor. 13:12). John, too, hints at our partial knowledge when he says, "It does not yet appear what we shall be, but we know that when he appears we shall be like him" (1 John 3:2). What this suggests is something that Paul also made explicit. The present age, including its knowledge and its prophecy, is bound by imperfection (1 Cor. 13:9). That imperfection reaches throughout the whole created order and undoubtedly at times includes also our ability to distinguish Christian from non-Christian phenomena. Even in our discerning of spirits we are often left with questions. As with all gifts, even claims to discern must themselves be carefully discerned. But by whom?

Discernment is a gift which is given to *the whole church*. It is given

---

29. Dunn, "Discernment of Spirits — A Neglected Gift," 85.

to enable the church to recognize claims of authenticity. Sometimes this may be accomplished through rational means alone, while on other occasions it may include trans-rational or "intuitive" means. The effectiveness of discernment may be improved through the use of both together. This judgment involves the whole church, even though some may be more gifted in this and may give leadership to the community in its discernment. The church, after all, is a *community of believers,* whose members are bound in relationship to all others (1 John 1:3, 6-7). Cyprian spoke out repeatedly against the idea of isolated Christians, claiming that there was no church apart from those gathered in unity with the bishop. There was no room for the idea of an invisible church nor for a schismatic church.[30] Visibility and invisibility, if such distinctions were to be made at all, were, it would seem, assumed to be coincidental.[31]

On the surface it may appear that the issue of what form a particular group takes is not all that important. But issues of form in relation to discernment are very significant. If Samuel Terrien's notion that people see and experience the hidden yet self-revealing God in different ways is right, there must from the outset be some flexibility in the forms in which we discern and celebrate God's presence. In Terrien's paradigm these forms arise from the fact that, for some, the ear acts as a gate to their experience of God. Thus, they tend to respond to the presence of God through the celebration of God's name, the need for sacred time, and an emphasis upon the preached Word and a clear ethical response. On the other hand, there are many whose eye more readily receives and perceives the presence of God. Their response may lead to an emphasis upon God's glory, the need for sacred space, and an opportunity for enthusiastic embrace of that presence in worship. If Terrien's claim that uniquely in Jesus Christ these two ways of recognizing and responding to God come together in a legitimate inseparable dialectic, we may come to recognize that a

30. Cyprian, *Epistle* 43.5.2; *Epistle* 33.1.1; and *On the Unity of the Church* (Treatise) 1.5 and 13.

31. The idea that the church was a mixture of wheat and tares drew heavily from Jesus' parable (Matt. 13:24-30), and led, perhaps inevitably, to an ecclesiology of visible and invisible churches. Cf. Augustine, *In Answer to the Letters of Petilian* 3.2-3. Cf. John Calvin, *Institutes of the Christian Religion* 4.1.7. Unfortunately, though, some segments of the church have pressed this idea to an extreme, and so defined the true church as basically invisible.

variety of form is essential to a truly ecumenical theology of the church.[32]

It may be the case that those churches which judged the early Pentecostals for their enthusiastic experience of the Holy Spirit did so because they experienced God primarily through the ear, through hearing. They were rationally oriented, rather than experientially oriented. However, their criticisms were not of the rational side, but of the experiential side of this movement; they decried Pentecostals as fanatics.[33] On the other hand, Pentecostals may tend to experience God primarily through the eye, or the "inner eye." They are trans-rationally or intuitively experiential rather than rationally oriented. Yet it is interesting, and I think significant, to note that Pentecostal criticism of pronouncements of the ecumenical movement are not so much of their experiential aspects, but of their rational pronouncements. The Assemblies of God, for instance, criticizes the ecumenical movement generally on rational or doctrinal grounds.[34]

Could it be that part of the reason we do not always discern the church when we meet it in each other is that we do not adequately discern the Spirit at work in our midst? We are, to be sure, limited

---

32. Samuel Terrien, *The Elusive Presence: Toward a New Biblical Theology* (San Francisco: Harper & Row, 1978), 127, 137-38, 422, 443.

33. See notes 5-8 above.

34. The statement in the Bylaws (Article VIII, sec. 11) of the Assemblies of God reads:

> The General Council of the Assemblies of God disapproves of ministers or churches participating in any of the modern ecumenical organizations on a local, national, or international level in such a manner as to promote the Ecumenical Movement because
>
> a. We believe the basis of doctrinal fellowship of said movement to be so broad that it includes people who reject the inspiration of Scripture, the deity of Christ, the universality of sin, the substitutionary atonement, and other cardinal teachings which we understand to be essential to Biblical Christianity.
>
> b. We believe the emphases of the Ecumenical Movement to be at variance with what we hold to be Biblical priorities, frequently displacing the urgency of individual salvation with social concerns.
>
> c. We believe that the combination of many religious organizations into a World Super Church will culminate in the Religious Babylon of Revelation 17–18.
>
> (But even so this is not be interpreted to mean that a limitation may be imposed upon any Assemblies of God minister regarding his Pentecostal witness or participation on a local level in interdenominational activities.)

during this age; but we often seem to judge one another not on the basis of the strength of God's self-revealing ways among us, but on the basis of the weaknesses of God's self-revealing ways among the other. These weaknesses, it turns out, are really often weaknesses in ourselves, which we try to suppress and thereby ascribe to the other.

It may be that we cannot properly discern the church because to date we have not properly discerned the Spirit. Our inquiry into the biblical usages of the charism of discernment raised issues which suggest the need for careful, prayerful judgment of personal claims and the variety of forms in which the Spirit might be present. And might this not also be true of the claims of the various Christian communities and church? But central to this, whether it be objectively or subjectively perceived, is the person of Jesus Christ, the head under whom the whole body functions.

Ask the latest convert to the New Age movement about the person and work of Jesus Christ. Ask her to talk about and/or live out what it means to be a disciple of Jesus Christ. Ask the same question and watch the lives of those who follow the ways of Hinduism or Buddhism. For all their similarities to Christian life in the Spirit, the differences emerge most significantly at precisely this point. The church is a community of the Spirit committed to the Lordship of Jesus Christ, whose presence is assured wherever two or three are gathered in his name (Matt. 18:20). And it is the Spirit of Christ who makes this possible. To discern or to find the church, therefore, we must first seek the Spirit who enables the church to live in light of the confession that "Jesus is Lord" (1 Cor. 12:3).

Chapter Three

The Spirit in the Worship and Liturgy of the Church

LORELEI F. FUCHS, SA, AND
LAWRENCE C. BRENNAN, C.M.

In this chapter we will focus on a study of the presence and activity of the Holy Spirit in worship, and more particularly in the church's liturgy. First we will examine briefly some of the historical, theological, and pastoral dimensions of this matter, and then we will look more closely at its biblical roots. The discussion will obviously reflect the Roman Catholic perspective of its authors, but we intend that its scope also be ecumenical.[1]

1. Because we are here focusing on pneumatology and the experience of the Holy Spirit in the worship of the church from a Roman Catholic perspective in particular and within the context of the Western church in general, we will not give attention to the richness of the Eastern liturgical tradition and its pneumatology.

Sister Lorelei F. Fuchs, SA, is an associate director of the Graymoor Ecumenical and Interreligious Institute where she staffs the Lutheran-Anglican-Roman Catholic (LARC) desk. Prior to her present ministry, she served in her congregations' houses of hospitality in Assisi and Rome, Italy.

Rev. Lawrence C. Brennan, C.M., was ordained a Vincentian priest in 1976 and received his doctorate in sacred theology at the Pontifical University of Saint Thomas Aquinas, Rome, in 1982. After serving in Roman Catholic seminaries in Chicago and Denver, he is currently academic dean and assistant professor of systematic theology at Kenrick-Glennon Seminary in Saint Louis, Missouri.

51

We begin with a preliminary definition of the words *worship* and *liturgy* so as to clarify the distinction between these two terms. A discussion of the place of the Holy Spirit in the theology and praxis of the church's worship then follows, using history as a framework of presentation. Here we trace the historical development of Christian worship and touch very briefly on the history of the liturgical movement. We conclude this section with a few thoughts concerning the implications of the churches' reception of a renewed understanding of the epicletic power and presence of the Holy Spirit in the church's worship. That Christian liturgy derives from ecclesiology, which itself derives from christology, both of which derive ultimately from *theology*, signifies that the Spirit's presence in the church's worship and liturgy must be understood in terms of this order, and not as an isolated occurrence. Such a pneumatology is both an assumption of this essay and its implicit thesis.[2]

On the Distinction between Worship and Liturgy[3]

The terms *worship* and *liturgy* are commonly and often ecumenically used interchangeably, sometimes virtually synonymously, as meaning the doxology believers render to God.[4] Like the terms *oikoumenē*, meaning the whole inhabited earth, the Greek *leitourgia*, referring to the action of the people, and the old English *weorthscipe*, signifying attribution of worth, value, or respect, these terms have secular origins and were gradually adopted by Christians to express salient features of their relationship to the trinitarian God whom they profess. Worship is the celebration of the redemption of creation, humankind's praise that the God who creates is the God who redeems. This celebration is both response to and expression of Christian redemption as the experience of receiving and sharing in the life of the trinitarian God: the God who is Father/Mother has saved creation in the life, death, resurrection, and ascension of the Son, Jesus the Christ, by the power

2. See the first chapter in this book by Father Thaddeus D. Horgan, as well as Father Lawrence C. Brennan's reflections later in this chapter on the biblical and pneumatological foundations for understanding the work of the Spirit in the present.

3. This part of the chapter (to p. 65) is drawn from a paper presented by Sr. Lorelei.

4. For a detailed treatment of these liturgical terms, see James White, *Introduction to Christian Worship* (Nashville, TN: Abingdon Press, 1980), esp. 22-28.

of their Holy Spirit, whose descent upon those who follow Jesus enables them to live as he did and so be united with the Godhead.

In describing the church's response of thanks and praise to God for this redemption, Roman Catholic theology makes a distinction between worship and liturgy. Worship is understood as the total "service of praise, adoration, thanksgiving and petition expressly directed to God in sacred signs and inward attitude."[5] Liturgy is, more particularly, the official worship of the church, the "official service of God offered by the mystical body of Jesus Christ, head and members."[6] Consequently, in the technical sense, liturgy here denotes specifically the official public worship of the church, her corporate ritual prayer of praise and intercession with God. The gathered assembly is the locus for liturgical prayer. Worship, on the other hand, is inclusive of a variety of expressions of adoration and veneration, and includes both shared and personal piety and devotions that complement formal corporate prayer. In the Roman Catholic tradition, liturgy is that worship which is authorized by the See of Rome and which takes place in communion with the local ordinary (bishop) according to the Roman See. While liturgy in the Roman tradition embraces litanies, novenas, the rosary, the stations of the cross, and prayers of intercession invoking the saints as mediators between the faithful and God, it focuses primarily on the communal celebration of Word and sacrament. This includes acts of baptism, confirmation, eucharist, reconciliation, anointing, marriage and orders, word services and the liturgical hours of lauds, terce, sext, none, vespers, compline, and the office of readings.

The specific definition of the terms *worship* and *liturgy* is thus connected with one's particular ecclesial tradition. Readers who are members of communions which share such worship forms as those mentioned above may view these terms as having to do with the distinction of the general (worship) and the particular (liturgy), which involves noting three corollary points: all liturgy is worship, but not all worship is liturgy; liturgy includes but is more than simply the eucharistic liturgy (the Mass); and liturgy includes those rituals officially authorized by the church, in distinction from those forms and rituals Christians may devise from time to time for a special purpose.

5. Karl Rahner, *Dictionary of Theology* (New York: Crossroad, 1990), 540.
6. Ibid., 280.

Readers in communions which do not have such worship forms as those referred to above may find it easier and more appropriate to use the terms *liturgy* and *worship* interchangeably.

The Spirit in the History of Christian Worship

The history of Christian worship shows that worship is a way in which the church expresses her identity and unity. With roots in the experience of the creative-redemptive Spirit of Yahweh[7] hovering over Israel as expressed in Israel's domestic and temple prayer, the worship of the first Christians was modeled on the liturgical gathering of the Jewish *berakah* and *zikkaron*, which included praising, thanking, glorifying, and acknowledging God for God's saving deeds *(berakoth)*, remembering these not simply as events taking place *in illo tempore* (only in the past) but also as the efficacious re-presenting of the past redemptive acts of God as a present reality *(zakar, zikkaron)*. The *todah zebach*, a sacrificial meal of *berakoth* for which Israel gathers to *zakar* (receive) salvation from death or from that which is life threatening, is the highest form of Jewish *berakah*, and thus it is a ritual, according to rabbinic tradition, that is to be celebrated throughout eternity. From pre-exilic, exilic, and post-exilic times continuing through New Testament Judaism, this liturgical observance served to confirm Israel's identity and strengthen their unity as the people of God, assuring them that the *ruach* (Spirit) of Yahweh was with them.

Having prayed in common through the spontaneous yet also structured ritual of the *berakoth* and having celebrated the *zikkaron* of feasts commemorating purification, atonement, harvest, and so on with Jesus, the first Christians continued this form of worship after his resurrection, including in the Christian *berakoth* Jesus' life, death, ascension, and outpouring of the Spirit. Through this form of worship they experienced the Spirit communicating the saving events of God. As the prophetic action of Jesus hosting a sacrificial meal on the night before he died on the cross acquired greater symbolic meaning among

---

7. Using her unpublished class notes, the author acknowledges lectures by Professor Paul Bradshaw and Father Regis Duffy, OFM, from the Department of Theology of the University of Notre Dame, as sources for this discussion of *berakah* and *zikkaron*.

his disciples, it was not long until Jesus' last supper was understood as the Christian *todah zebach*. An outline of the liturgical shape of the Jewish *berakah* and that of early Christian common worship demonstrates the similarities of the two liturgies as well as the spirit of their worship:[8]

Jewish Berakah	Early Christian Liturgy
berakoth; blessing God	praise of God
narrative remembering of God's deeds	anamnesis of God's deeds
petition	petition; intercession
chatimah; praise	doxology

By the middle of the second century, Justin Martyr delineates a similar outline of Christian worship, while adding some specific Christian elements. He describes a word service followed by a eucharistic service on Sundays and implies that the eucharistic liturgy no longer takes place within the context of a meal as did the Jewish ritual and earlier Christian celebration. He lists these elements:

- introductory praise of God
- readings of Scripture recalling God's deeds
- preaching by presider
- common prayer
- [if the eucharist is celebrated, transfer of gifts and preparation of the table
- eucharistic prayer (anaphora with epiclesia and amen)
- [fraction and communion]
- doxology, with trinitarian reference
- almsgiving
- [communion taken to those not in attendance][9]

Hence the shape of the church's worship is in place early on, but with a freedom of spontaneity and space typical of the *berakoth* to pray *ex tempore*. The early Christians' belief in Jesus and their experience of

---

8. For an explanation of the parallels of Jewish liturgical prayer and prayers in early Christianity, see Paul Bradshaw, *Daily Prayer in the Early Church* (New York: Oxford University Press, 1982).

9. This outline is gleaned from Justin's *First Apology,* chaps. 65-67.

oneness in his Spirit led the Christian community to develop its prayer with variety, so intimate was the relationship of their life and liturgy. The worship of the early believers emerged out of their deep sense of *koinōnia* (community/communion) in God's Spirit, whom they experienced primarily during worship. Pentecost, the coming of the Holy Spirit, was understood as a "decisive moment in the beginning of the church";[10] and every worship thereafter embodied in its praise and thanks this outpouring of the Spirit. It is the presence of the Spirit that makes Christ's community the temple of God, a spiritual building where true spiritual sacrifices are offered and where worship in spirit and truth occurs.[11]

As trinitarian theology develops in response to the christological and pneumatological controversies of the fourth and fifth centuries, what was generally accepted belief and received liturgical praxis is attested to in patristic writings and creedal formulae: the Holy Spirit's sanctifying power is experienced in the church's worship, particularly in the liturgies of baptism and confirmation; and the Holy Spirit is worshiped and glorified together with the Father and the Son.[12] In theology as well as in the life of the community, then, the Spirit is confessed to be the principle uniting and vivifying the church and the church's Word and sacraments.[13]

Yet, the implicit assumption and explicit expression of the Spirit-filledness of early church life and liturgy — the Pentecostal *pleroma* experience of the felt presence of God by a persecuted sect of highly committed believers — seemingly fade in the Western church as she experiences a shift in relationship with the world around her. It is a shift that changes her identity, and hence also her worship. From the skepticism and persecution experienced in the early apostolic and sub-apostolic period, to tolerance and establishment of the church in the Constantinian era and later under the reign of Charlemagne, through the Middle

10. Frederick Cwiekowski, *The Beginnings of the Church* (New York: Paulist Press, 1988), 71.

11. See 1 Peter 2:5 and John 4:23-24.

12. On the significance of the Holy Spirit in early trinitarian theology, see Basil, *On the Holy Spirit;* Gregory of Nazianzen, *Oration 31;* and the Nicene-Constantinopolitan Creed of 381.

13. Among the most significant expositions of pneumatology in sacramental theology is the work of Father Edward Kilmartin, S.J. See his *Christian Liturgy I: Theology* (Kansas City: Sheed and Ward, 1988).

Ages, with the growing tension of the *filioque* controversy which even-tuated in the East-West schism, and later the polemics of the sixteenth-century Reformation with its arguments not only over doctrine but also over liturgy and sacraments, evidence of the pneumatological and epi-cletic dimensions of worship generally receded. The church's worship tended more to model the performance of courtly ceremony, or-chestrated by a clericalism that elicited an increasingly passive role of spectator on the part of the faithful. Notwithstanding the vast diversity of rites that developed in the church up to and beyond the sixteenth century,[14] the church's liturgy tended to give little explicit recognition to God's Spirit as an experience of *communio/koinōnia*. Rather, the liturgy increasingly became the work of a select few for the benefit of the many. It was to this that both the Reformers and the Council of Trent tried to respond — unfortunately, however, given the polemical climate of the time, not always within the most positive context, as such terms as *protest(ant)*, *counterreformation* and *anathema sit* denote.

In the Roman Catholic Church, the post-Tridentine liturgical reforms mandated for the first time standardization of liturgical texts and rubrics for pastoral use throughout the entire Roman church in an effort to retrieve the spirit of worship. In Protestant worship, Martin Luther sought to purify what he called "use of abuse" and to free the church from its "Babylonian captivity."[15] With the intention of fol-lowing the discernment of the Spirit's leadings for reform and renewal, reformers and counterreformers often pitted Word against Sacrament, thus crafting new Christian worship forms. Both, however, sought to preserve the apostolic faith and to retrieve sacred words and actions of the church with the enlightenment available at the time, but without the benefit of historical-critical scholarship of later centuries and the conciliatory milieu of the present.

14. For treatment of rites such as the Ambrosian, Gallic, Gallican, and Roman and their diversity, see White, *Introduction*, and Cheslyn Jones, Geoffrey Wainwright, and Edward Yarnold, S.J., eds., *The Study of Liturgy* (New York: Oxford University Press, 1978).

15. The two notions quoted are common in Luther's liturgical reform. The former, *abusus not tollit usum*, reveals a conservative approach to change in worship. The latter, in an essay of the early Luther on *The Babylonian Captivity of the Church* (1520), addresses three distorted understandings of the eucharist as practiced in the Roman Catholic Church in the sixteenth century: the explanation of the mass as a present sacrifice, the withholding of the chalice from the laity, and the use of the word "transubstantiation" to describe the change in the elements.

For almost four hundred years the churches have gone their separate liturgical ways, with minimal or no interchange. But supported by modern biblical and ecumenical movements, the liturgical movement seeks a reversal in this praxis via the recovery of worship as the experience of the paschal mystery of God's creation and redemption of humankind through Jesus Christ the Son by the power of the Holy Spirit.

While the churches of the Reformation pioneered the biblical movement, the liturgical movement has developed from origins in the Roman Catholic Church in mid-nineteenth-century France. Dom Prosper Guéranger, a Benedictine monk, began refounding monasteries at that time which were to become centers of the revitalization of the church's worship so that the church could reclaim worship as central to her life and mission. Assisted by such timely papal documents as Pius X's *Moto Proprio Tra Le Sollecitudini*,[16] which calls for a return to liturgy as the indispensable source of Christian life and for the active participation of the worshiping assembly, and by a series of congresses, which called for returning liturgy to the heart of Christian spirituality and recentering Christian life in the liturgy, the liturgical movement has sought theologically and pastorally to retrieve the Spirit in the liturgy, so that, to paraphrase the day's liturgical scholars, the *piété de l'eglise* (the piety of the church) may renew the *ecclesia orans* (the prayer of the church) in its proclamation of the *mysterium tremendum* of God.[17] The liturgical movement reweds after long separation life and worship by pastorally revisiting theology, christology, pneumatology, and ecclesiology. In doing so, it focuses attention on dimensions of Christian experience that the ecumenical world calls "Faith and Order" and "Life and Work" via the Christian experience of worship. Focusing on trinitarian theology and these ecumenical dimensions, a cloud of liturgical witnesses emerges after Guéranger in

---

16. *Tra Le Sollecitudini* was published on the 22nd of November 1903.

17. Lambert Beaudin used the phrase "piety of the church" in a book of the same title published in 1914 to refer to the spiritual life of the church that is fostered in Roman Catholic liturgy. *La Piété de l'Eglise* was translated as *Liturgy, the Life of the Church,* and appeared in English in 1926. *Ecclesia Orans* was a series begun in the German Benedictine monastery of Maria Laach in 1918, which produced works that addressed liturgy and liturgiology from historical, theological, and pastoral perspectives. Its first issue included Romano Guardini's *The Spirit of the Liturgy*. Odo Casel adopted the phrase *mysterium tremendum* in his controversial theology of *kultmysterion* which was developed in the *Jahrbuch für Liturgiewissenschaft,* founded in 1921.

the late nineteenth century and into the twentieth century as precursors to the major implementation of the reform of Christian worship initiated at the Second Vatican Council.

Sociological consciousness was brought to the liturgical movement by another Benedictine monk, Lambert Beauduin, who used his pastoral ministry as a chaplain worker-priest to put into effect the teaching of *Rerum Novarum*.[18] While launching a renewed worship which would lead to Christian living and witness of not only monks, clergy, theologians, and intellectuals but also of faithful Sunday churchgoers, Dom Beauduin's lead was supported and followed by many. Romano Guardini insisted upon the importance of the intention and participation of worshipers in the act of worship, complementing the *kultmysterion* theological foundation given liturgiology by Dom Odo Casel. Scattered throughout Germany, France, and Austria, monasteries and other institutes served as centers for a reform of worship that would serve to reform the church, in the hope that the church would in turn reform society. A liturgical apostolate spread abroad to the Anglophon world. In the United States, a grass-roots experience of worship as the center of church life and as the source of her missionary activity began at St. John's Abbey in Collegeville, Minnesota, under the inspiration of Father Virgil Michel, and was shared by the ecumenical Liturgical Conference in Washington, D.C., the Catholic University of America, and the University of Notre Dame's Department of Theology and Center for Pastoral Liturgy.

The experience of celebrating the liturgy in the underground resistance during World War II strengthened the sense of worship as a resource for forming religious identity and solidarity. One need only remember the lives and ministries of Maximillian Kolbe and Dietrich Bonhoeffer to see the powerful effects of such awareness. The promulgation of Pope Pius XII's *Mystici Corporis* and *Mediator Dei* around this time[19] also gave momentum to reform and renewal of Roman Catholic worship, which would later influence decisions at the Second Vatican Council, and which also assisted the ecumenical movement in reception of convergences in worship and common liturgical texts among the churches. The focus of *Mystici Corporis* on ecclesiology

18. *Rerum Novarum,* Pope Leo XIII's encyclical on Roman Catholic social teaching, was published in 1893.

19. The date of *Mystici Corporis* is 1943, and that of *Mediator Dei* is 1947.

provided pastoral complications for the church's worship; and *Mediator Dei,* which focused mainly on worship, gave cautious but affirmative support to the liturgical movement developing in the Catholic Church since the time of Guéranger. This same pope had already supported the biblical movement, affirming it officially in the encyclical *Divino Afflante Spiritu,*[20] despite considerable resistance in some quarters of the church to critical Scripture scholarship.

Thus, by looking at worship through a historical lens, we see more clearly the trinitarian dimension of Christian liturgy and particularly the movement of the Holy Spirit calling the church to be more fully the church theologically and pastorally in the context of history. The anamnetic and epicletic, whether made explicit as in the early church or implicit in her liturgy as the church grew in time and space, is that which gives life to the Christian *koinōnia.* It is the spirited remembering of a people in relation to God. This is the spiritual climate in which the Second Vatican Council opened and in which it promulgated as its first document *Sacrosanctum Concilium,* the *Constitution on the Sacred Liturgy.*[21] The council identified the liturgical movement and the ecumenical movement as movements of the Holy Spirit within the church.[22] *Sacrosanctum Concilium* describes worship in terms of the axiom *lex orandi, lex credendi,*[23] the notion that the law of worship establishes the law of belief, meaning that we express our belief in our worship, that worship is a norm of faith, a witness to the apostolic faith received and celebrated by the praying church. The church, as the body of Christ formed by the Spirit as God's people, identifies herself as such when she worships the trinitarian God who creates, redeems, and sanctifies her and all creation. Through worship in word and sacrament, the church remembers Jesus Christ and receives his Spirit, who communicates his continued presence in history. At the same time, in the guidance and power of the Spirit the church professes her hope in God's new, creative manifestation of the future kingdom. Hence the trinitar-

20. *Divino Afflante Spiritu* was published the 30th of September 1943.

21. The Second Vatican Council opened on 11 October 1962; *Sacrosanctum Concilium (SC)* was promulgated on the 4th of December 1963.

22. See *SC* 43 and *Unitatis Redintegratio* 3, 4, in Austin Flannery, OP, ed., *Vatican Council II: The Conciliar and Postconciliar Documents* (Northport, NY: Costello, 1987).

23. For the origin and explanation of the fifth-century axiom *legem credendi statuat lex supplicandi,* see McBrien, *Catholicism* (San Francisco: Harper & Row, 1981), 28, 541.

ian dimension, and specifically the pneumatological, gives Christian worship its distinctively eschatological character: in worship the church remembers, praises, and thanks God for the love of the Holy Spirit who "eternally binds" Jesus the Redeemer to the Father Creator and who "flows out" from the Father through the Son to gather and scatter creation for life and mission on the way to at-one-ment in God's reign.[24] Consequently, it can be said that

> it is the liturgy through which . . . the "work of redemption is accomplished"; and . . . through the liturgy . . . the faithful are enabled to express in their lives and manifest . . . the mystery of Christ and the . . . nature of the church. . . . The liturgy daily builds up . . . the church [making her] a holy temple of the Lord, dwelling place for God in the Spirit . . . [increasing her] power to preach Christ. . . .[25]

In Christian worship the church gathers to celebrate the mystery-presence of Christ by the power of the Holy Spirit gifted to us by God the Father/Mother for life and mission.

Conciliar and postconciliar liturgical reform has coined and uses the term *paschal mystery* for what is at the center of all Christian worship.[26] Christian paschal mystery is reception of the God who creates as the God who redeems through the life, death, resurrection, and ascension of Jesus, and through the descent of God's Spirit at Pentecost. Christian worship as a whole celebrates that paschal mystery, which the *Constitution on the Sacred Liturgy* teaches is both the cause and goal of redemption:

> The Paschal Mystery is, therefore, not only the cause of the salvation of the world but also the goal: the gathering of all into Christ, the Lord of history, and so into union with the Father in the Spirit. The

24. Mary Collins, OSB, "Liturgy," in *The New Dictionary of Sacramental Worship,* ed. Peter Fink, SF (Wilmington, DE: Michael Glazier Books, 1990), 594.

25. *SC* 2.

26. For a detailed treatment of the notion of "paschal mystery," see Edward Kilmartin, SF, "The Sacred Liturgy: Reform and Renewal," in *Remembering the Future, Vatican II and Tomorrow's Liturgical Agenda,* ed. Carl Last (New York: Paulist Press, 1983); also, Robert Taft, S.J, *Beyond East and West: Problems in Liturgical Understanding* (Washington, DC: Pastoral Press, 1984). See also the documents on the sacred liturgy in Flannery, ed., *Vatican II,* particularly *SC* 6, 10, 47, 48, 102-8; *Inter Oecumenici* 6.

Paschal Mystery is the origin, foundation and goal of the Church. This Holy People of God and Body of Christ participates now in the Paschal Mystery. It already shares, by way of anticipation, in the fulfillment of the Kingdom of God yet to come.[27]

Already but not yet it is the gathering of all into Christ, the Lord of history, so that all may be brought into union with the Father and the Son in the Spirit, which will only be fully achieved in the eschaton.

The liturgy, more specifically, and, in Roman Catholic understanding, especially the eucharistic liturgy, is the experience via ritual celebration of participation in the paschal mystery by anticipation, a foretaste of the fulfillment of the coming kingdom. This participation in the paschal mystery requires of the church growth in the fullness of Christ by dying and rising with him and drawing others to herself by the power of the Spirit working in and through her so that God may truly be "all in all." All the activity of the church has the function of continuing the revelation and realization of the work of redemption accomplished by God through Christ in the power of the Spirit. The liturgy, and indeed all Christian worship, is **part** — the central part — of this activity. *Sacrosanctum Concilium* describes the liturgy as the most expressive manifestation and realization of the work of redemption. It is the "summit toward which the activity of the church is directed" and the "fount from which all her power flows."[28] Consequently, following the principle of *lex orandi, lex credendi,* it may be said that the pneumatological in worship shapes the church's missiological role and defines her eschatological character. That is to say that the very faith, order, life, and work of Christians are established and guided by the Spirit's action through the church's worship. Furthermore, since Christian worship celebrates the paschal mystery — creation's redemption in Jesus' life, death, resurrection, ascension, and the descent of the Spirit — it becomes the means through which the Spirit completes through them the redemption proleptically experienced in the liturgical act of worship. Christian living is the movement of the Spirit in the lives of the faithful as the extension of the epicletic movement of the Spirit in Christian worship. The Holy Spirit realizes (makes real) in the gatherings and scatterings of Christians the redemption of the world that is celebrated in Christian liturgy and worship. Hence, it is rightly said that

27. Kilmartin, *Remembering,* 36.
28. *SC* 10.

The One who gathers the assembly for worship is, in the end, the Spirit. The One who is the ultimate teacher of the faith is the Spirit working in the hearts of believers. The Spirit's tools are the community, its common worship, its acts of service. Let the liturgy, the worship of the church, do its work. And then may we confirm that work in acts of worshipful service to the larger world.[29]

Thus, to understand and express more clearly the role of the Holy Spirit in the worship of the church calls for encouragement of diversity in ways of liturgical renewal and for responsible cultural and pastoral adaptation in liturgical praxis. Active participation of the laity in the liturgy; Christian education which fosters understanding of the significance of the functions and symbols which liturgy includes;[30] creative use of art, environment, music, dance, movement, and the *ex tempore* in worship; and revised, more inclusive common liturgical texts and rites can serve to form a Spirit-filled body and can better embody the Spirit experienced by worshipers gathered around pulpit and altar to hear and proclaim the Word, celebrate the hours, break the bread, and share the cup.

Within and among the churches creative energies are already at work responding to the challenge to which this movement of the Spirit calls the church. Yet the greater ecumenical challenge of this pneumatology of the worship of the church and how this is expressed in the churches still awaits consideration. What is our communal worship in the Spirit? Word services, sacramental celebrations, liturgical hours, devotions, and the worship of two or more gathered in God's name are all avenues of the Spirit — but how does the Spirit unite us and draw us toward those who worship differently than we do? That the Holy Spirit enables the church at worship to affirm communally what God has done in Christ (redemption) for humankind (creation) challenges all of us and also the churches to press toward a better ecumenical understanding of the implications of such a pneumatology based in Christian worship. This is so because, paradoxically, it is worship, the "locus" of the deepest unity among the churches, that is also precisely the "focus" of their

29. *Liturgy: The Christmas Cycle*, vol. 9, no. 3 (Washington, DC: The Liturgical Conference, 1991), 12.

30. Liturgical functions include acolytes, cantors, crossbearers, lectors, ministers of communion, and ministers of hospitality. Liturgical symbols include such things as candles, incense, vestments, movement, and resources for art and environment.

disunity.[31] Recognizing the presence of the Holy Spirit in other churches, and in other ecclesiologies, therefore, leads us also to ask, How is the Spirit to be recognized in other churches' liturgies and worship? And to what extent are the churches receptive to receiving the Holy Spirit through another's worship, liturgy, and sacraments?

More specifically, if, as *Baptism, Eucharist and Ministry* states, Christians receive the Holy Spirit and are incorporated into the body of Christ at baptism,[32] why is there inability among some churches to recognize others' baptisms as sharing in the one baptism in Christ? Baptism into Christ only occurs via baptism in one of the churches of Christ. Furthermore, if baptism is incorporation into the body of Christ and sharing in the body of Christ is sharing in eucharist, why do some eucharists excommunicate certain baptized members? Epiclesis of the Holy Spirit over gifts and assembly to sanctify both can be the univocal claim of no one church. What is the meaning of the recent growth in Christians' awareness and experience of the Holy Spirit, be it in the Pentecostal movement, charismatic renewal, or the Spirit and spirits involved at the Seventh Assembly of the World Council of Churches in Canberra in 1991? Can the Lima liturgy,[33] precisely because it is the liturgy of no *one* tradition, become a liturgy for *all*? Or does its very extradenominational status mean that it is therefore outside the liturgical theology and praxis of churches moving toward a common *lex orandi* and *lex credendi*? Cannot the unity-in-diversity of the *koinōnia* of the Spirit manifest in the churches include a diversity of liturgical praxis in our different ways of celebrating the paschal mystery, and thus model a Spirit-guided diversity-in-unity in and for the human community?

Historical, pastoral, and theological reflection upon the interplay of ecclesiology, pneumatology, and liturgy reveals the organic bond that exists between the renewal of worship and the renewal of the whole life of the church. The church's worship is central to the church's self-expression. *Legem credendi statuat lex supplicandi:* wor-

---

31. As Margaret Mary Kelleher, OSU, points out in Fink, *New Dictionary,* p. 385.

32. See "Baptism" in *Baptism, Eucharist and Ministry,* Faith and Order Paper No. 111 (Geneva, Switzerland: World Council of Churches, 1982), sec. II C, 203.

33. For the text and information on the eucharistic liturgy composed for the Faith and Order Conference held in Lima, Peru, in 1982, see Max Thurian and Geoffrey Wainwright, eds., *Baptism and Eucharist, Ecumenical Convergence in Celebration,* Faith and Order Paper No. 117 (Geneva, Switzerland: World Council of Churches, 1983).

ship is the basis of the church's theology. The church lives by her liturgy and draws from it strength for her life and mission. For Christian worship to be what it truly is, therefore, it must be worship in the Spirit, a *kairos* experience of the Holy Spirit (see John 4:23-24). As such, it impels Christians into the *chronos* of worshipful service to the faith community and to the wider human community. Christian worship calls the Christian *oikoumenē* to a common pneumatology that recognizes and receives the experience of the Spirit groaning within us. When this is more epicletically evidenced in all our worship, we will be thrust by the Spirit of God into greater visible unity with diversity, in both faith and order, in life and work, so that "all may be one . . . so that the world may believe . . ." (John 17:21).

But does this have an even broader biblical base than only this oft-cited text from the Gospel of John?

Biblical Roots of Worship in the Movement of the Spirit[34]

The church's experience of the Spirit through worship does indeed have deep and broad biblical roots, and tracing these is important in discerning how the Spirit works through the church's worship today and its leading toward the future.

First of all, we should note that Jesus of Nazareth was often in prayer. On the mountain as evening came (Matt. 14:23-24), very early before dawn in a deserted place (Mark 1:35), through the hours of the night (Luke 6:12), in solitude accompanied by his disciples (Luke 9:18), he prayed. As was the custom of his people, he went to the synagogue on the Sabbath (Luke 3:16), and from his childhood he seems to have participated in temple worship (see Luke 2:41-51); in any case, he recognized the temple as a house of prayer (Matt. 21:13). In his exultancy at the return of the seventy-two, he is said to have rejoiced in the Spirit and praised the Father of the lowly (Luke 10:21). After his baptism by John, it was while he was praying that the Holy Spirit descended in the form of a dove and a voice came from heaven (Luke 3:21ff.). On another occasion, it was while he was praying on the mountain with Peter, James, and John that he was transfigured,

---

34. The remainder of this chapter is based on a paper contributed to the study by Fr. Larry Brennan.

and the voice came from heaven revealing him to his disciples (Luke 9:28ff.). On both occasions, the voice affirmed him as the Son of God.

At the climax of what would be his final meal on earth, Jesus raised his eyes to heaven, he celebrated his union with his Father, and he prayed for his disciples (John 17:1-26). In the darkness of Gethsemane, troubled and distressed, he pleaded with his Father, his *Abba,* that he might be spared from his approaching death; yet he surrendered his will to the will of the Father. From the cross, he cried out to the God who had seemingly forsaken him; yet he prayed to God to forgive his tormenters (Luke 23:34), and he finally entrusted his spirit to the one he addressed as *Abba* (Luke 23:46).

Not only did Jesus himself demonstrate a life of worship and prayer in the Spirit, but on one occasion, when he had finished praying, one of his disciples asked him, "Lord teach us to pray." In response, he taught them the Our Father, or Lord's Prayer. But that prayer did not direct attention only beyond himself, for when, at the Last Supper, Philip asked him, "Master, show us the Father, and that will be enough for us" (John 14:8), Jesus, who had just asserted that he was the way to the Father, affirmed that to have seen him is to have seen the Father (John 14:9), so close is their interworking. The Gospel here indicates most explicitly the close, inseparable bond between the Father and the Son (John 14:20). And since Jesus goes on to indicate that he is also in his disciples and they are in him (John 14:10), it follows that they will know the Father through him. Even more, he goes ahead of his disciples to seek for them another Advocate, the Spirit, who will lead them into all truth (John 15:13).

It is by the power and guidance of the Spirit that his disciples are to pray, with confidence in Jesus' promise, "Ask, and it will be given to you" (Matt. 7:7ff; Luke 11:9-13), "so that your joy may be complete" (John 16:24). Jesus told parables of the friend at midnight (Luke 11:5-8) and the persistent widow (Luke 18:1-7) to reinforce his instruction. The writers of the New Testament continued such instruction, telling believers to persevere in prayer (Rom. 12:12; Col. 4:2), to pray at every opportunity (Eph. 6:18), to pray without ceasing (1 Thess. 5:17) night and day (1 Tim. 5:5), continually offering to God a sacrifice of praise (Heb. 13:15).

The intercession of believers parallels and reflects that of Jesus himself in glory, who lives forever to intercede for those who approach God through him (Heb. 7:25; 9:24; see Rom. 8:34; 1 John 2:1). In the same way, the Spirit that Christ has sought for us and has given to us also intercedes for us, "for we do not know how to pray as we ought" (Rom. 8:26). Since both Jesus and the Spirit intercede for us, both are called advocates (see 1 John 2:1; John 14:16). Moreover, insofar as the intercession of the church is joined to the intercessions of its advocates, it grows in strength and efficacy, for without them we can do nothing (see John 15:5). In this way Christ's prophecy is fulfilled; those who are born of water and the Spirit (John 3:5) worship the Father in Spirit and truth (John 4:23-24).

We, too, are to pray in the Spirit (Eph. 5:18; 6:18; Jude 20), and that same Spirit inspires in us the prayer of God's children, for through the power of the Spirit we are "adopted" as God's children and through the Spirit we cry, "Abba! Father!" (Rom. 8:15; see also Gal. 4:6), as did Jesus the Son.

That we are adopted in the Son through the Spirit defines an important pattern in Christian worship. Christ offered himself to God through the eternal Spirit, and the blood of Christ cleanses us for worship of that same God (Heb. 9:13-14). Thus, through Christ, we have access in one Spirit to the Father (Eph. 2:18); and through Christ we are to continually offer to God a sacrifice of praise, the fruit of lips that confess his name (Heb. 13:15). Filled with the Spirit, we are to give thanks to God in the name of Christ (see Eph. 5:18-20). We can approach God with confidence, knowing that, through Christ and in the Spirit, we have first been loved (1 John 4:10) and sought (see Matt. 18:10-14) by this very God.

This last point is of primary importance. The liturgy and worship of the church take place not primarily at our initiative but at God's. In John's Gospel, Jesus tells us, "No one can go to the Father except through me" (John 14:6), and "No one comes to me unless the Father draws him" (John 6:44; see 6:37, 65). Similarly, he says, "And I — once I am lifted up from the earth — will draw all people to myself" (John 12:32). This idea of drawing seems related to the testimony of God on Sinai, "I bore you up on eagle's wings and brought you here to myself" (Exod. 19:4; see Deut. 32:11); that is, God bore the people to Sinai that they might offer sacrifice to God and enter into covenant with Yahweh. In the new covenant, the Father bears us up on the wings of the Spirit to Jesus, for no one can acknowledge Jesus except in the Spirit (1 Cor. 12:3; 1 John 4:2-3; see Rom. 8:9). Thus, through Jesus and in the Spirit, the Father draws us into eternal life with the triune God (1 Cor. 15:28; see 1 Cor. 5:19).

Begotten of water and the Spirit

But you were washed, you were sanctified, you were justified in the name of the Lord Jesus Christ and in the Spirit of our God. (1 Cor. 6:11)

As all the Gospel accounts make clear, Jesus was baptized at the hands of John. This Jewish rite of ablution, purification, or initiation had been transformed by John into a baptism of repentance. Jesus, who was without sin (Heb. 4:15; 1 Pet. 2:22), in accepting a baptism of repentance, affirmed through this act his solidarity with sinners (Rom. 8:3; 2 Cor. 5:21; Gal. 3:14; cf. Deut. 21:23 and Heb. 2:27). And in so doing, he set the stage for the vicarious atonement that would consummate his life and ministry. Though Christ was innocent, he assumed our guilt and its penalty, thereby averting that penalty from us.

In the imagery of the baptism narratives, the Spirit descends on Jesus in the form of a dove. This image evokes the memory of Noah and the end of the Flood, which the Lord had brought about to destroy earth's wickedness. Baptism is thus seen as the "flood" that destroys sin and brings new life, which is symbolized in Genesis by the olive branch returned by the dove (Gen. 6:11). In the baptism narratives, a voice is heard from heaven, saying, in Matthew's account, "This is my beloved son, in whom I am well pleased" (Matt. 3:17). In Mark's and Luke's accounts, the voice speaks in the second person (Matt. 1:11; Luke 3:22). In all three accounts, there is clear reference to an enthronement psalm, Psalm 2:7, and to the opening of the first Servant Song, Isaiah 42:1. Later, in the transfiguration of Jesus, which is an anticipation of his Easter glory, there is heard the same voice and a similar message (Matt. 17:1-8; Mark 9:2-8; Luke 9:28-36; cf. 2 Pet. 1:17), with the added injunction, "Listen to him." The voice is at once a revelation of Jesus' unique relation to the Father and an anticipation of the Father's intention to glorify his Messiah-Son.

Thus, the liturgical feast of the baptism of the Lord is a feast of divine manifestation, the prototypical epiphany. For in the baptism narratives we see the revelation of the Father, Son, and Spirit, making themselves known in their respective saving roles. Nevertheless, the revelation of the Trinity is not an end in itself nor a supreme riddle to test our faith: it is rather the revelation of a mystery in which we come to know not only the triune God but ourselves as well — saved by this gracious God. Thus, the baptism narratives show, right from the beginning of Jesus' public ministry, what the passion and resurrection narratives will show at its end: the Father, who loves the Son and has sent him for our salvation; the Son, who loves the Father and accepts from the Father the mission to save us; and the Spirit, who is sent by the Father and Son, putting an end to sin and bringing new life.

In John's Gospel, as Jesus dies on the cross, he "hands over" the spirit (John 19:30), a verbal nuance that suggests more than simply breathing his last. Earlier in this Gospel (see John 7:37-39) Jesus had already promised the Spirit to any who came to him to drink living water. The evangelist now adds the observation that this gift of the Spirit would be linked to Jesus' glorious return to the Father. In a similar way, on the evening of the first day of the week, when the risen Jesus first appears to the disciples (John 20:9-23), he shows them his hands and side still bearing the marks of his passion. He then sends them, as the Father had previously sent him. And in doing so he breathes on them, and says, "Receive the Holy Spirit. Whose sins you forgive are forgiven them, and whose sins you retain are retained" (John 20:22-23).

These two incidents, Jesus' passion and his commissioning of his disciples, are inseparable. As Jesus dies on the cross, his last breath releases the gift of the Spirit. Water and blood, the symbols of baptism and the eucharist, the very life of the church, flow from his opened side. As Jesus rises in glory, he stands before his disciples still bearing the wounds of his passion. He breathes on them, and so confers the Holy Spirit to empower them for the forgiveness of sins, the soul of his redeeming work.

When the Spirit comes upon the church, and particularly in its worship, the Spirit comes as the Spirit of the Father through the Son, and puts into effect in the church what has been given from the Father in and through the Son. Paul tells the Corinthians,

> And we all, with unveiled face, beholding the glory of the Lord, are being changed into his likeness from one degree of glory to another; for this comes from the Lord who is the Spirit. (2 Cor. 3:18)

That is, the Spirit who came forth from Jesus on the cross, from the risen Jesus in the upper room, from the glorified Jesus at the right hand of the Father, is the Spirit that, especially in worship, makes us like Jesus in his *kenosis* and his glory. Paul instructs the Romans that we who have been baptized have been baptized into the death of Jesus so as to be united with him in the resurrection (see Rom. 6:3-11). Moreover, as the death of Christ was a death to sin, we are consequently to consider ourselves "dead to sin and alive to God in Christ Jesus" (Rom. 6:11). As the grain of wheat must first fall to the ground and die before yielding its fruit (cf. also John 12:24), so those who sow to the Spirit "will from the Spirit reap eternal life" (Gal. 6:8). The God who raised Christ from the dead will raise us also from the dead, through the Spirit who dwells in us.

We receive already a foretaste of this in the eucharist, in which we are

Given to drink of one Spirit

> On the last and greatest day of the feast, Jesus stood up and exclaimed, "Let anyone who thirsts come to me and drink. Whoever believes in me, as Scripture says: 'Rivers of living water will flow from within him.'" He said this in reference to the Spirit that those who came to believe in him were to receive. (John 7:37-39)

The eucharist is first and last the living memorial of Christ. When, in the eucharist, we eat and drink, it is not just bread and wine we receive but Christ himself (see John 6:53-58). Yet the New Testament provides us with two passages, one each in John and Paul, that suggest that in this eucharistic act we receive the Spirit as well. Whereas normally it is said that in the symbols of the eucharist, Christians partake of the body and blood of Christ, these passages speak of believers drinking of the Spirit (John 7:37-39; 1 Cor. 12:13; see Heb. 6:4). Admittedly, these texts do not suggest an explicit reference to the eucharist; however, it could be reasonably suggested that the eucharist is connoted in the language used. Why would John and Paul speak of drinking of the Spirit? In a sacramental context, the water that the authors describe would normally be considered the water of baptism; but we do not drink of water at baptism. It is rather the wine of the new covenant given in the eucharist that we drink.

The study of religion has taught us that religions sometimes put symbols to unusual uses, and that symbols themselves often combine in order to emphasize an underlying meaning. In this case, elements of two sacramental symbols are fused: water is substituted for the wine

of the new covenant, the wine that is the blood of Christ. Thus, in
the fused symbol, in drinking of the Spirit through the baptismal water,
we are led to drinking of Christ in the eucharistic wine. A similar
fusion, for example, occurs in the book of Revelation, where one of
the elders, speaking to the seer, says of the saints, "They have washed
their robes and made them white in the blood of the Lamb" (Rev.
7:14). Here, the fused — and jarring — imagery of washing in blood
parallels and complements the imagery of drinking of the Spirit: the
water of baptism in which we bathe is juxtaposed with the blood of
the Lamb, the blood of the covenant; thus in the fused symbol we are
washed in Christ's blood with the cleansing agent of the Spirit (received through the baptismal water).

Together the two symbol fusions demonstrate the essential link
between baptism and the eucharist: we drink the wine of the new
covenant, the blood of Christ, having been previously inaugurated
into that covenant by the waters of baptism — waters in which we
ourselves die with Christ to rise to new life in the power of the Spirit.

Insofar as the eucharist is the living memorial *(anamnesis)* of
Christ, it is the celebration of the presence of Christ in his total reality,
including his birth, life, death, resurrection, and glorification, and his
sending of the Spirit. Semantic studies have taught us that this
memorial is not a mere calling to mind, but an effective rendering
present. The Jewish feast of Passover is a memorial in a similar sense
(Exod. 12:14; 13:3-10; see Deut. 16:3). But in the eucharist, the
Spirit is the effective power of remembrance. In John's Gospel, Jesus
says to his disciples:

> The Counselor, the Holy Spirit, whom the Father will send in my
> name, he will teach you all things, and will bring to your remem-
> brance all that I have said to you. (John 14:6)

That is, the Spirit will do more than simply remind us of what Jesus
said and did long ago; the Spirit will bring about the reality that the
words of Jesus signified, namely, salvation. This is the "remembrance
of me"[35] that Jesus promises his disciples in Paul's account of the

---

35. In the Johannine passage, the Greek reads *hypomnēsei;* in the Pauline passage,
the Greek reads *anamnēsin.* Both terms, however, are derived from the root *mnē,* and
both would fall within the semantic field of the Hebrew *zkr,* with its overtones of
memorial as actualization. See C. Brown and K. H. Bartels, "Remember, Remem-

institution (1 Cor. 11:23-26), which is summarized by a Pauline formula that has itself become a part of the liturgy: "As often as you eat this bread and drink this cup, you proclaim the death of the Lord until he comes" (1 Cor. 11:26).

The Christ who is rendered present in this memorial is the glorified Christ, yet one who still bears the wounds of his passion, the living symbol of his self-gift. The Spirit whom he sends us from the Father, in this same paschal mystery, is the Spirit of their mutual self-gift. It is both a life-giving force (see John 6:63) rendered present by the memorial and the power by which the memorial renders present what it signifies (John 14:26).

Thus in the eucharist precisely as we remember Jesus we must also ask for the Spirit. The celebration of the eucharist from earliest times included a prayer, called the *epiclesis*, that the Father send the Spirit; it is the most prominent pneumatic feature in the liturgy. In a sense, this prayer echoes that of Christ himself, who asks the Father to send us the Paraclete (John 14:16), and encourages us to ask for this as well, in his name. This prayer, by all who offer it, is always answered by the Father (see Luke 11:13).

In this same Spirit, the washing or baptism of regeneration and renewal takes place (Tim. 3:5), bringing about a new creation in Christ (see 2 Cor. 5:17; Eph. 2:15). Indeed, the principal feature of this new creation is the reconciliation brought to us by Christ, a reconciliation through which the old things have passed away and new things have come (2 Cor. 5:17, after Isa. 43:18-21; see Rev. 21:1-5). The Spirit comes as a power that transforms. For this reason, in much of Christianity the eucharistic *epiclesis* is linked to the transforming power of the eucharist, a transformation that affects the bread and wine, and the congregation that celebrates the eucharist, and even, as focused in these elements, the universe itself.

Finally, the eucharist is a communion in the body and blood of Christ (1 Cor. 10:16-17). The body of Christ, the church, is animated by the Spirit (1 Cor. 12:1-31), who gives gifts for the good of all (1 Cor. 12:7). Again, as Paul tells the Corinthians, we are one body through the one eucharistic loaf; and even more fundamentally, we are one body in the one Spirit through the one baptism (see 1 Cor.

---

brance," in *The New International Dictionary of New Testament Theology*, vol. 3, ed. C. Brown (Exeter, Devon, UK: Paternoster Press, 1978), 230-47.

10:16-17; 12:12-13). It is by the gift of the Spirit in baptism and the eucharist that Christ's priestly prayer is accomplished: "May they be one, Father, as you are in me and I in you, that they may also be in us" (John 17:21). For fellowship in the Spirit is nothing less than a participation in the fellowship of the Father and the Son.

Conclusion

As Christ the Son offered himself to the Father through the eternal Spirit, so through Christ in the same Spirit we have access to the Father. Moreoever, this access is made possible by God's salvific power. Without the mediation of Christ and the power of the Spirit, our worship would be of no avail.

The baptism of Jesus was a baptism into death, removing the penalty of sin and communicating the saving love of the Father and the Spirit. In a similar way, our baptism is a baptism into Christ's death, in which we receive the same Spirit and are raised by the same Father to newness of life. That life is above all a life of service and worship, reflecting the servant obedience of the Son, who emptied himself for our sakes, and who on that account was exalted by the Father, and from whom we receive the Spirit which makes us participants in his self-emptying and obedience.

The eucharist is thus inseparable from baptism, and the two together are made effective through the power of the Spirit. As Jesus washed the feet of his disciples at the Last Supper, so, at the Lord's Supper in the church, we are to continue to render service to one another in the Spirit. It is through the Spirit that we offer the thanksgiving that is the heart of the eucharist. It is through the Spirit that we effectively remember Jesus in the eucharist and participate in his saving death and resurrection. Finally, in our communion in the body and blood of Jesus through our shared remembrance, we are animated by the Spirit and united by the Spirit, in accordance with the prayer of Jesus that all be one as he and the Father are one. Such unity is the essential glory of the Father and the Son, and as the Spirit leads us into it, the Spirit leads us in giving glory and worship to God.

Chapter Four

The Spirit in the Proclamation of the Church

GEORGE VANDERVELDE AND WILLIAM R. BARR

Where — and how — is the Holy Spirit active in the church's proclamation of the gospel? Let us begin this inquiry by considering the proclamation of a specific local congregation (while recognizing that the Spirit also works through the proclamation of the church on regional, national, and international levels as well). The congregation we have in view is not some ethereal ideal congregation but one that struggles in its particular situation to proclaim the gospel faithfully.

The Church as Proclaimer of the Gospel

Grace Church is a suburban church of some three hundred members located in an area of slowly integrating housing. Most of its members, however, are white and middle class; and though the church has an "open door" policy, it has not made much effort to reach out and invite persons of other racial and ethnic backgrounds and economic status into its membership. Most of the members are socially and

George Vandervelde, of the Christian Reformed Church, teaches in the Institute for Christian Studies in Toronto, Ontario, Canada.

William R. Barr, a member of the Christian Church (Disciples of Christ), teaches theology at Lexington Theological Seminary, Lexington, Kentucky.

economically upwardly mobile, although a growing number have been
laid off through recent plant closings and cutbacks.

The church has an extensive program of activities in addition to
worship and church school. It has a day care center, a program for
the elderly, interest and prayer groups, and an evangelism task force.
Some of its members are active in local programs for the homeless
and hungry; several are involved in the local Habitat for Humanity
project of building homes for and with those in need.

How does this congregation proclaim the gospel? In the largest
sense, the very existence of the congregation and its life as a whole is
both a witness to and proclamation of the gospel. Since the gospel is
the good news of redemption and renewal in Jesus Christ, this also
includes the community of faith that carries on this proclamation.
Thus, Grace Church is itself a small part of that good news story. But
it is this only because Christ himself is present in it through the power
of the Spirit. For that reason, the members of Grace Church can be
called "living letters" of Christ written by the Spirit of God (2 Cor.
3:2-3). As a member of this community, Joan Scott shows that she is
such a letter as she nails down a piece of plywood for the floor of the
new Habitat home; and Steve Murray demonstrates that he, too, is
such a letter as he puts his brush to a newly stretched canvas that is
to evoke something of the puzzle and wonder of life.

In the stricter sense, however, proclamation is what the church
"says" in and to its situation, its explicit articulation of the gospel in
its particular social context. This occurs most obviously by means of
words: the reading of Scripture, preaching, teaching, evangelizing, and
prayer. But in a broader sense it occurs also in what the church says
as it lives its life and in its reaching out to others in the community.
In the character and quality of its life as well as in its words and actions
it proclaims the good news of God's salvation and mediates God's call
to new life in Christ. Not that this occurs perfectly or unambiguously
in its life. The congregation periodically surveys its life and programs
and evaluates them, and strives to make all the facets of its life more
effective and authentic means of proclamation. Let us examine more
closely how the Spirit is involved in this.

The Church — Created by the Spirit

First of all, the church is that community called into being by the proclamation of the good news of Jesus Christ, who is himself present in it by and through his Spirit. Through hearing and trusting this gospel, the Christ-community is formed, sustained, and constantly called to account. Grace Church is part of this worldwide community of Christ. While it is true that the church was humanly planned and organized, namely, by a group commissioned from First Church downtown to form a new congregation, its roots go much deeper. Its existence as part of the church of Jesus Christ is ultimately a work of the Spirit. By its very existence the church both proclaims and lives by the power of the Spirit: the Spirit who is both the power and implementer of the gospel. Thus, as the apostle says, "Faith comes from what is heard" (Rom. 10:17; cf. Acts 2). Indeed, the basic reason the church is called into existence is to proclaim this good news. Yet it does this not simply by its own intention and action but under the guidance and with the help of the Spirit of God. "Spirit" here is more than simply a name for those ideals that unite this group around a hero of the past who is believed to have exemplified such ideals. Rather, the Spirit of God that creates this community makes present the living Christ within its midst (John 14:18, 26). As this occurs, God calls together — actually calls into being — the church, fills it with faith and life, and sends it out in mission to proclaim the gospel to all.

In this way the Spirit begins a process aimed at the total transformation of life. As Luther puts it, through the Spirit the word of proclamation "drives Christ into the heart." Through the work of the Spirit in the lives of persons and in the life of the church, human lives are changed; the Spirit works a radical transformation (in the sense of reaching to the roots) of human life. Classically this is spoken of as conversion, regeneration, sanctification, rebirth, and filling with the Holy Spirit. The Holiness movement has especially emphasized this aspect of the Spirit's work, but other church traditions also have had to take account of this facet of the Spirit's work, whether they speak of it more in terms of spirituality, sanctification, renewal, or change of perspective.

The Spirit-createdness of the church is decisive for every aspect of the church's life — for its order, its worship, and its proclamation. In its proclamation the church explicitly acknowledges that it lives by

the Spirit of God, which is also the Spirit of Christ, that is to say, by
the Spirit by which God creates, sustains, judges, and works to heal
the world. At the same time, it proclaims that through Christ, God
has poured out the Spirit in a new way, creating the church to proclaim
the good news of salvation in Christ. Yet in proclaiming this, it must
also acknowledge that this is the same Spirit who spoke through the
prophets and was active in Israel's life, giving it its distinctive character,
and which is working even now to bring Christians and Jews into
dialogue.[1] To put it in the language of the classical affirmation of the
church, it is the Spirit who "proceeds from the Father through the
Son," or who "proceeds from the Father and shines out through the
Son," who enlivens and empowers the church in the proclamation of
the gospel.[2]

But if we are to see more clearly how the existence of the church
is integral to its proclamation and the role of the Spirit in this, we
must consider more closely what it means to be the church. In the
New Testament, the term "church" is sometimes used in a more
restricted sense to refer to the Christian community gathered in worship. Wherever people are gathered in Christ's name, as in Grace
Church, there is the church.[3] Thus, when the church gathers for
worship it also proclaims whose it is and what it is. It does so as it
engages in open, explicit dialogue with God, a dialogue which includes

---

1. As stressed in current ecumenical discussion around the theme "Toward a
Common Expression of the Apostolic Faith Today"; see Hans-Georg Link, ed., *One
Lord, One Spirit: On the Explication of the Apostolic Faith Today,* Faith and Order Paper
No. 139 (Geneva: World Council of Churches, 1988), 105-17. Also, see *Confessing
One Faith,* Faith and Order Paper No. 140 (Geneva: World Council of Churches,
1987), 25-26; and *The Theology of the Churches and the Jewish People* (Geneva: World
Council of Churches, 1988).

2. See the important convergence between Eastern and Western churches on
this as expressed in the "Klingenthal Memorandum" (1979), the text of which can be
found in Hans-Georg Link, ed., *Apostolic Faith Today: A Handbook for Study,* Faith
and Order Paper No. 124 (Geneva: World Council of Churches, 1985), 231-44. For
an ecumenical discussion of the significance of this statement, see Lukas Vischer, ed.,
Spirit of God, Spirit of Christ, Faith and Order Paper No. 103 (Geneva: World Council
of Churches, 1981). For a discussion of its significance for the North American church
context, see Theodore Stylianopoulos and S. Mark Heim, eds., *Spirit of Truth* (Brookline, MA: Holy Cross Orthodox Press, 1986).

3. The significance of this simple, yet foundational, truth is explored in a fine
article by Miroslav Volf, "Kirche als Gemeinschaft," *Evangelische Theologie* 49 (1989):
52-76.

prayer, praise, and proclamation. But while all of this is certainly human activity, it becomes authentic proclamation of the gospel only as it occurs in the power of the Spirit, the Spirit who "intercedes" between Christ and us (Rom. 8:27), and who ultimately enables and sustains this dialogue and proclamation.

The church does not, however, cease to proclaim the gospel when communal worship ends. This points to the proclamation of the church in a larger sense. For the church includes the whole life of the community (the *koinōnia*, communion) of those who profess Christ; and this includes its life and witness not only as a gathered community but also as dispersed into the world. In other words, the church also exists wherever Christ through the Spirit is present among his people in their daily activities. And since all our activity is communicative in one way or another, proclamation, in this larger sense, takes place through the lives and actions of all the church's members. Hence, when the community leaves worship and its members return to their homes, take up their work, engage in the arts, serve those in need, and so on, proclamation continues but in different — and not only verbal — ways. But it is important to note that here too the Spirit is working, enabling Christians to declare and live the good news of the redemption of the world in Christ.

The Church as the Concrete Manifestation of the Spirit

In its proclamation, the church attests not only that it is a creation of the Spirit but that the Spirit also continues to manifest itself in its life. This occurs not only in what the church says verbally but also in the way it lives. As a community in which there are varied gifts, persons of different backgrounds and experiences and with different interests, talents, and abilities, the church itself manifests the creative activity of the Spirit which it announces to the world (1 Cor. 12:4ff.). The main reason, therefore, that Grace Church should strive to be a more inclusive community of people of varied backgrounds is that the community in its varied life is, as Paul says, the temple of the Holy Spirit (1 Cor. 3:16-17).

Yet this does not necessarily mean that the church is always a model of peace and harmony. There certainly can be, and often are, differences and tensions within the community. And there is also much that is sinful and wrongheaded within this community, as it should be the first to confess. But it should show by the way it deals with such tensions that it lives by the Spirit of God's forgiveness and correction. That, of course, can never be simply taken for granted but is to be received joyfully and lived out afresh ever and again. The credibility of the church's proclamation of God's forgiveness in Christ hinges on whether it takes this good news seriously in its own life and lives in its power.

In this way the church "embodies" its proclamation in its own life. But this does not mean that the Spirit is something the church possesses in such a way that the Spirit is at the church's disposal or under its control. The Spirit is always God's *gift* filling the church, transforming, reforming, and renewing it, and sending it forth in power. As the church proclaims the gospel through its life in the power of the Spirit, it becomes in effect the mouth of Christ, the "oracle of God" (1 Pet. 4), through whose voice God makes appeal to all.

This communication is addressed not only to the cognitive level of human being but to the affective and spiritual levels of human being and relationship as well — indeed, to every dimension of human life. Studies in a number of areas, including more recent hermeneutics, are helping us see more clearly the polyvalent nature of language and religious symbols.[4] Words and images communicate on a number of levels at once; and the Spirit works on these many levels in and through human communication to lead and draw people more deeply into truth. Thus, for example, when members of Grace Church care for one another, when they speak truth to one another, when they speak the gospel to those beyond their walls through their concern and outreach to the community, they articulate the Christian message in ways that speak its meaning in many ways and on many levels. And when they, and other groups of Christ's followers, address in his name the urgent problems of our time — such as pollution, depletion of natural resources, wanton destruction of the unborn, violation of human rights, discrimination against minority groups, exploitation and

---

4. See, *inter alia*, on this, Joseph Campbell, *The Mythic Image* (Princeton, NJ: Princeton University Press, 1974); Mircea Eliade, *Images and Symbols* (New York: Sheed and Ward, 1961); Philip Wheelwright, *The Burning Fountain*, new and rev. ed. (Gloucester, MA: Peter Smith, 1982); Paul Ricoeur, *The Rule of Metaphor* (Toronto: University of Toronto Press, 1981); and Janet Schaffran and Pat Kozak, *More than Words* (Oak Park, IL: Meyer-Stone Books, 1988).

marginalization of the poor, the physical and psychic abuse of spouses and children, and the moral and spiritual disarray evident in much of our society — the church also articulates the gospel in the power of the Spirit.

True, there are differences among the churches, as well as differences among the members within them, as to precisely how the gospel is to be defined and nuanced and lived out in today's world. But underlying these differences is a widely shared agreement that Jesus Christ is at the center of the Christian gospel and shapes all of its content. The Spirit, who comes from Christ and through Christ, works to make the gospel of Christ effective in the life of the church and in the world. Authentic proclamation of the gospel does indeed involve sharing the suffering of the world — but in the power of a word that can redeem life and make it whole.

The church's statement of the gospel through word and act is thus at once a work undertaken in the power of the Spirit and a concrete manifestation of the Spirit. Yet, as we have seen, this speech is highly varied. Proclamation occurs in all the facets of the church's life. It occurs not only through preaching and teaching but also through the service of the members of Grace Church as they live and work in the community. Indeed, wherever people serve in Christ's name in the arts, academia, or politics, they are part of the church's proclamation of the gospel. In fact, at times people directly involved in such activities may be better equipped to speak pertinently, to be a voice of the Spirit to their particular audience, than those officially appointed by the church to preach and teach. But the essential point is that the good news is best served when all share in its proclamation, each according to her or his particular abilities and opportunities. The Spirit works through many channels and in many ways to empower persons to speak faithfully and effectively the gospel in their situations.

The Spirit Empowers the Proclamation of the Gospel

The Spirit, then, creates a community that exists as part of the ongoing story of Christ. Such a community is most truly itself in passing on this story. And while this occurs focally in the worship and teaching of the church, what happens there also brings into focus the transforming power of proclamation in other areas of the life of the church as well. In the church's worship the Word of God is read, proclaimed, and acted out. And though those who lead the service have a special role to play in this, all members of the church share in the proclamation of the gospel through worship.

Here the priesthood of all believers should be concretely manifested and exercised. Instead of relegating the act of proclamation only to a few, worship should include all the people in the articulation of the gospel. All God's people are to "prophesy" (Acts 2:17-18), that is, are called to proclaim the story of God's love (1 Pet. 2:9). Worship ought to be conducted in such a way that, whether it is led by one person or a few, others have ample opportunity to participate verbally as well as through music and bodily movement. Black churches and Pentecostal churches have much to teach the rest of the church in this regard.[5] If, however, the gathering is so large that responses by the community are not easily evoked, alternative ways can be found to enable and encourage the participation of all in the proclamation of the gospel. Not only does this "involve" people in such a way that they can better hear and appropriate the gospel themselves, it also expresses and communicates the power of the gospel to permeate the life of all and to draw all into the service of Christ. But this cannot be achieved simply through human organization and methods of involving people in the life of the church; it comes about ultimately through the power of God at work in and through the lives of people, in and through the life of the church, making actual here and now the new formation of life in Christ.

Here again it is important to note that the proclamation of the church is not limited only to the work of those trained and appointed as professional ministers or clergy. Certainly they have an important role to play in this, but proclamation occurs also through Christians, groups, and the church as a whole, as they speak and live the gospel in specific situations. More specifically, proclamation occurs through their words, actions, the quality of their lives and their life together, and through their presence in the world. In such proclamation they not only point to a past event, a Jesus long ago and far away, but they

5. See, e.g., on the contributions of African-American churches, David T. Shannon and Gayraud S. Wilmore, eds., *Black Witness to the Apostolic Faith* (Grand Rapids, MI: Eerdmans, 1985); James H. Cone, *The Spirituals and the Blues* (New York: Seabury Press, 1972); and on the contribution of Pentecostal and charismatic churches, Frederick Dale Bruner, *A Theology of the Holy Spirit* (Grand Rapids, MI: Eerdmans, 1970), esp. chap. 3.

show forth one who is present and who presents himself in the Spirit through their life and witness. Their calling is to display and declare in the totality of their lives and life together the mighty work of the one who called them out of darkness into the light (1 Pet. 2:9-10).

Yet, while every member of the church is called by grace to be a proclaimer of the gospel, some are especially gifted for leading and guiding in this task. They should be encouraged to use this talent and gift in teaching or preaching to aid the whole community in proclaiming the gospel. Whether ordained or not, their leadership is important in helping the community articulate the gospel in a clear and relevant way in the contemporary situation. Those who have had the opportunity for seminary study and training have a special responsibility to help equip all Christ's followers to participate in telling of him. The Spirit works through them, but is not limited only to them; rather, as in the early church, the Spirit is poured out on everyone, the entire church of Christ, so that it may be equipped — ever more fully — to be proclaimers of the gospel.

Discerning the Spirit Within and Beyond the Church

At the same time, the church proclaims not only that the Spirit is active in its life but also that the Spirit transcends its life. This is manifested first of all in the critical or tensive relation of the Spirit to the church. The church must constantly test itself in the light of the good news it is called to proclaim — as, for example, the gospel challenges the timidity of Grace Church in reaching out to and making minorities feel welcomed into its membership. Such testing necessarily entails spiritual discernment: the recognition in faith of the Spirit's activity and the responsiveness of persons to the leading of the Spirit. This is possible only because the Spirit works through the church's proclamation to inform, guide, counsel, judge, and renew the community of faith itself — and to empower it in God's mission. The critical testing of the church by the Spirit occurs both through continuing study of the Scriptures and through informed involvement in the needs of the world, for it is precisely at this juncture that the Spirit opens to us more fully the meaning of the biblical witness and leads us to discern more clearly what does and what does not comport with the Word of God as revealed in Scripture.

Although every member of the church is called to be involved in such discernment of the Spirit, the carrying out of this task is differentiated among the members and among the church's various official ministries. There are those who are especially gifted for and formally called to the teaching of the faith, and they have a special duty to guard and transmit the faith once for all delivered to the saints. But this is achieved most fruitfully when the teachers and proclaimers are closely bound to the community they serve and are responsible to the community, welcoming and acknowledging its gifts of discernment. Through such discernment the church itself is made accountable to the Spirit. And in this way the Spirit works through the proclamation of the church to make this proclamation more adequate and powerful in reaching people both within the community and beyond it.

But the Spirit is not confined to the church. In the largest sense, the Spirit is the presence and activity of God in the world. Hence if it is this Spirit that is active through the church's proclamation, then that proclamation will have to help its hearers recognize more clearly the Spirit at work in the whole of creation (including human culture and society). While all members of the triune God share in this work (as the ancient writers said, the *opera trinitatis ad extra sunt indivisa:* the outwardly directed works of the Trinity are indivisible), the particular work of the Spirit is that of creating, sustaining, transforming, unifying, and leading creation to its ultimate end in praise and service of God (Ps. 33 and Rom. 8).

At the same time, the Spirit's redemptive mending of creation involves also convicting the world of sin (John 16:8-11) and of our own blindness in rightly discerning the Spirit's work. Thus, while the presence and activity of the Spirit in the world must be affirmed, we must also acknowledge that it is often difficult to discern precisely how and where the Spirit is acting in the world. The Scriptures call for a discernment and sorting out of the "spirits" (1 John 4:1). The need for this indicates the mixed and often contradictory forces at work in our situation; what may appear to us right and helpful may, on closer examination, turn out to be tied in with forces and structures of evil that oppress and do injury to ourselves and others in the world.[6]

6. As Christians and others in other parts of the world are helping us in North America see more clearly. See, e.g., Leonardo Boff and Virgil Elizondo, eds., *Option for the Poor: Challenge to the Rich Countries,* Concilium, Vol. 187 (Edinburgh: T. & T.

Should we say that all activity that leads to greater well-being of the creation is directed by the Spirit of God? That surely is one criterion, but it seems that other criteria must be considered as well, such as whether the activity really exposes the true nature of our division and transforms as well as makes creation whole. Also, the Spirit works to transform the "heart," to make human life new at its center and in its depths, for, as Jesus pointed out, good fruit can come only from a good tree (Matt. 7:16-20). At the same time Jesus stops short of the simplistic reversal of this: good deeds automatically indicate good people (Matt. 7:11). Rather, the aim of the Spirit is not only to produce good deeds but also to change the human spirit which finds expression in such deeds. Furthermore, amazingly, the Spirit works to turn what was meant for evil to good (Acts 16:19-34).

In its proclamation the church should help people recognize and respond to the work of the Spirit in the world and to oppose whatever is not of the Spirit of God. Even though the world often fails to recognize the Spirit and regards its work in secular terms, the church should help people see, for instance, that the rising cry for freedom and justice is part of God's Spirit-led design for humanity. Insofar as movements for human solidarity, protection of the environment, and empowerment of the disenfranchised give expression to the formation of true human community in love they are to be discerned as movements of the Spirit in our time. At the same time we also have to recognize that such movements are always influenced by other "spirits" which are often in tension with God's Spirit. For instance, "freedom and equality" can be construed to mean absolute human autonomy, that is, concern for one's (or a group's) own well-being in disregard of or to the detriment of the well-being of others. Even advocacy of human rights can at times become myopic and cause us to overlook the wider connection of human life with the rest of creation, the "rights" of creation as well as of human beings to protection and fulfillment in God's love for the world. God's Spirit struggles against other "spirits" of our time to lead us to a larger

---

Clark, 1986); Penny Lernoux, *Cry of the People* (Garden City, NY: Doubleday, 1980); James H. Cone, *For My People* (Maryknoll, NY: Orbis Books, 1984); and Robert McAfee Brown, ed., *Kairos: Three Prophetic Challenges to the Church* (Grand Rapids, MI: Eerdmans, 1990). See also Hans-George Link, ed., *Confessing Our Faith around the World* (Geneva: World Council of Churches, 1983-84).

vision of the connection of justice and the integrity of creation. Struggles for liberation in which God's Spirit is at work can become distorted into the means of one group gaining domination over another; equality can be distorted into anarchy, and solidarity into a bland uniformity which discourages individuality. Living in a conflictual situation, the followers of Christ must struggle to discern what is truly of the Spirit of God — as revealed in Christ — and what is not, and must commit themselves to live by the Spirit of Christ, seeking to embody love in a just society.

"It Seemed Good to the Spirit and to Us"

One dimension of the church's proclamation of the gospel and the work of the Spirit in it has to do with decision-making. The process of decision-making in the church as well as the specific decisions that are made should concretely proclaim the good-news story the church is called to communicate. But too often decision-making in the church is guided more by concern with management techniques to ensure the survival of the institution than by a clear connection to the content of the gospel that this institution was established to serve. Grace Church, for example, can get so preoccupied with a fund-raising drive for the renovation of its building that it short-changes its outreach to the growing numbers of needy in the community. When this happens, decision-making is obviously determined more by immediate pragmatic considerations than by prophetic vision and pastoral insight. It is instructive to recall in this connection how the New Testament church, when faced with day-to-day decisions concerning its life and vision, did not simply ask what seemed "practical" or self-serving. Rather, it placed the issues carefully and prayerfully in the light of God's mission as focused in Christ and being implemented through the Spirit. Only in that context could they conclude what "seemed good to the Holy Spirit and to us" (Acts 15:29). However, the Spirit's counsel did not come out of the blue but concretely in relation to the proclamation of the good news of Jesus Christ. This determined the priorities in terms of which the Spirit led the church in its decision-making and implementation. Apart from that leading with its focus in Christ, the church's decision-making all too easily falls into various forms of legalism and coercion "from above" — an above, it should be noted, that is *not* of the Spirit!

The Identification of the Spirit through Proclamation

In the activity of the Spirit in and through proclamation, the Spirit is also identified and revealed more fully. As Gregory the Theologian put it: "the Spirit is what [the Spirit] does."[7] What this says is that in its work the Spirit reveals itself as not merely an appearance or temporary manifestation of God but as the reality of God present in our midst as one who draws us into community with God and others through Christ. The Spirit is able to do this because the Spirit shares in the community of eternal life in God.

But how more particularly is this self-identification of the Spirit to be understood? The Spirit is often viewed as rather nebulous or faceless. Even at Pentecost, when the church was born in a "gale" of the Spirit,[8] the Spirit is imaged as like a wind or fire that comes from heaven. But though the Bible speaks of the Spirit at times as an energy or force, it also speaks of the Spirit in more personal terms, as teaching, counseling, interceding, defending, and admonishing the Christian community. And though the Hebrew and Greek terms for spirit, *ruach* and *pneuma,* are neuter, the Bible often uses these terms in ways that suggest personal activity and identity (Ps. 143:10; Isa. 34:16; 63:10; Ezek. 3:12; Mark 1:12; Acts 8:29, 11:12; Rom. 8:16, 26).

But if the Spirit is to be understood as personal, is the Spirit also characterized by gender, or is the Spirit really ultimately genderless? People often think of the Spirit, if not as a "he," then as a general power, as an "it." But the work of the Spirit is often described in Scripture in terms of feminine characteristics, such as giving birth, nurturing, guiding, and sustaining. Furthermore, the Spirit is linked with or identified with *Sophia* in the Wisdom literature and in the Septuagint.[9] Should the Spirit then be thought of as "she"? While this would express more clearly the feminine qualities of the Spirit —

---

7. *Theological Orations,* 5.29.

8. See esp. John Calvin's exegesis of Acts 2:1-4 in his *Commentary on the Acts of the Apostles,* vol. I, ed. David W. Torrance and Thomas F. Torrance, trans. W. J. MacDonald (Grand Rapids, MI: Eerdmans, 1966).

9. For more on this, see Joan C. Engelsman, *The Feminine Dimension of the Divine* (Philadelphia: Westminster Press, 1979), esp. chap. 5; also, Elisabeth Schüssler Fiorenza, *In Memory of Her: A Feminist Theological Reconstruction of Christian Origins* (New York: Crossroad, 1987), esp. 130ff.

who is frequently spoken of as the "mother" of Christians, giving them life, nurturing and guiding them[10] — it nevertheless might suggest that the Godhead is only one-third feminine, as it were. It seems truer to the biblical portrayal of God to recognize that God's activity is characterized by both feminine and masculine traits, and that, ultimately, God is beyond sexual differentiation and certainly beyond our stereotypical images of male and female. Nevertheless, the partnership of male and female may well express an important aspect of the image of God, namely, of the God who enters into community and communion with us out of community and communion of the triune persons within God's own life.[11] Because the Spirit shares in the triune life of God in equality and communion and empowers such life in those among whom it works, the Spirit is manifested among us in the development of a community of women and men united in complementary responsibility. Jesus' relations with others, both women and men, shows that what God intends and creates in and through Christ is a community in which there is mutual respect, affirmation, love, and service. The Spirit continues the work of creating such community and because it does so, the Spirit may be spoken of in masculine and feminine terms, so long as neither is used exclusively and it is recognized that God finally transcends our human images and concepts.

The Spirit — In Whom We Are One

This leads to a further insight. The Spirit is revealed in the proclamation of the church as the one in whose power the church is one. When we recognize another person or another community as part of the church, this entails the recognition that the Spirit that recreates and

10. As Yves Congar notes in his *I Believe in the Holy Spirit* (New York: Seabury Press, 1983) 3:161-62.

11. As Dietrich Bonhoeffer already suggested in his incisive essay *Creation and Fall* (London: SCM Press Ltd., 1959), but more recently developed at length by Leonardo Boff, *Trinity and Society,* trans. Paul Burns (Maryknoll, NY: Orbis Books, 1988). On the important ethical implications of this, see, in addition to Boff, Douglas John Hall, *Imaging God* (Grand Rapids, MI: Eerdmans; New York: Friendship Press, 1986). See also Janet Crawford and Michael Kinnamon, eds., *In God's Image* (Geneva: World Council of Churches, 1983).

vivifies the other is the same Spirit that vivifies us, is in fact the one Spirit that unites us in Christ. Our unity in the Spirit is not simply a feeling, nor an abstract theological concept, but the presence of God we actually experience in our encounter with other Christians in worship, service, and care for one another. It is what enables us to recognize and confess that we share in the body of Christ, that Christ is the center and goal of our life, and that empowers us to proclaim the good news of Christ in and to the world.

As we begin to recognize this and take it seriously, we can no longer tolerate a divided church. We see more clearly how much the division of the church contradicts its very proclamation. If, as we noted at the beginning of our inquiry, the church is the creation of the Spirit through Christ, then to live in separation from one another and in indifference to one another as churches is to deny the very Spirit which has called us into being. If the church is the creation of the Spirit, then the existence of insular churches is itself a "grieving" of the Spirit. Just as there are no private "hook-ups" through the Spirit between isolated individuals and Christ, so there are no private connections through the Spirit between isolated, and alienated, churches and Christ. The Spirit calls into being the one church; and the Spirit works within the church to reunite it.

Yet we cannot deny that the Spirit has worked and given different gifts in our various churches and church traditions. We would also deny the Spirit if we did not take these gifts appreciatively and offer to share them with one another. And as we do this in the power of the Spirit, the Spirit may also lead us to a new and larger vision of what the church may become as a community that cherishes and draws upon these gifts in the Spirit's leading.

Such an approach to unity via the Spirit offers a number of hopeful prospects. First of all, it expands our vision of the church to include the whole people of God.[12] Thus, it represents what might be called an ecumenism "from below," that is, from the roots from which the church springs. By beginning with the Spirit, we perceive that many of the issues that are now considered to be the prime church-dividing issues, though by no means pushed aside, are

---

12. And thus also requires and motivates Christians to engage in interfaith dialogue, as was emphasized particularly at the recent Assembly of the World Council of Churches at Canberra.

nevertheless ultimately relativized, including such continuing barriers as ministry and sacraments. As important as such issues are, they are finally not as important as the true and basic communion *(koinōnia)* that exists among us in the life of the Spirit. Would that our life together as churches made this more clearly visible among us!

Chapter Five

The Spirit in the Formation and Forms of the Church

WILLIAM R. BARR AND HORAND GUTFELDT

While it may be in some respects easier to feel and to recognize the Spirit in the worship and proclamation of the church, some may find it more difficult to discern the Spirit in the structure of the church — in its order, organization, procedure, and ways of decision-making and implementation. Yet from the beginning of the Christian movement the Spirit has been perceived in forming as well as transforming the community of faith in God's mission (e.g., Acts 2; 4:32–5:11; 6; etc.). Nevertheless, the actual formation and development of the early Christian community is complex, and it is not always clear in this process what is of the Spirit and what is not, nor how to judge between conflicting claims to the Spirit.[1] Also today there are differences among

1. See Eduard Schweizer, *Church Order in the New Testament* (Naperville, IL: A. R. Allenson, 1961); Dom Gregory Dix, *Jurisdiction in the Early Church* (London: Faith House, 1938, 1975); Adolf von Harnack, *The Constitution and Law of the Church in the First Two Centuries*, trans. F. L. Pogson (London: Williams & Norgate/New

William R. Barr, a member of the Christian Church (Disciples of Christ), teaches theology at Lexington Theological Seminary, Lexington, Kentucky.

The Rev. Dr. Horand Gutfeldt, of the Swedenborgian Church, now retired, served for several years as head of the Greater Berkeley Interfaith Council, Berkeley, California.

Christians as to the presence and activity of the Spirit in the patterns and structures of the church's life, and at times tension is experienced between the movement of the Spirit and the institutional structures of the church.[2]

We propose to examine this complex issue here by first looking briefly at how the Spirit is perceived as working in and through the organization of the church in several different church traditions, and then on the basis of this review we will conclude with some more general reflections on the activity of the Spirit in forming, reforming, and renewing the structure of the church. In an effort to represent something of the range of the variety of different patterns of church order, our examples are drawn from two of the older churches, the Eastern Orthodox and Roman Catholic communions, from two churches with roots in the Protestant Reformation of the sixteenth century, the Lutheran and Presbyterian traditions, and from two North American-born churches, the AME Zion Church and The Church of God (Anderson, Indiana).

The Eastern Orthodox Church

The Orthodox Church is really a family (more than simply a federation) of self-governing or "autocephalous" churches, consisting of the four ancient Patriarchates (of Constantinople, Alexandria, Antioch, and Jerusalem) as well as eleven other regional or ethnic churches (of Russia, Romania, Greece, Czechoslovakia, etc.).[3] In addition, it includes several "autonomous" churches which are not yet entirely self-governing, in Finland, China, Japan, South America, and Australia.

York: Putnam's Sons, 1910); Hans von Campenhausen and Henry Chadwick, *Jerusalem and Rome: The Problem of Authority in the Early Church* (Philadelphia: Fortress Press, 1966); and William George Olson, *The Charismatic Church* (Minneapolis: Bethany Fellowship, 1974).

2. See, e.g., Jürgen Moltmann and Hans Küng, eds., *Who Has the Say in the Church?* Concilium, Vol. 148 (New York: Seabury Press, 1981); Cardinal Leon Joseph Suenens, *Coresponsibility in the Church,* trans. Francis Martin (New York: Herder and Herder, 1968); and Rosemary Radford Ruether, *Women-Church* (San Francisco: Harper & Row, 1985).

3. In addition to those mentioned these include the Orthodox churches of Serbia, Bulgaria, Georgia, Cyprus, Poland, Albania, and Sinai.

All share a common allegiance to the seven early ecumenical councils and to the authority of the living tradition manifested in the life of the church and particularly in its liturgy. Since the liturgy as a whole, and within it focally the celebration of the eucharist, is believed to be the means of Christ's presence in the power of the Spirit, the local congregation is seen as manifesting the church in its fullness. Thus the local congregation is said to be not simply a part of the church, but as a community gathered around its bishop and in unity with the church through the ages, it is believed to be the manifestation of the church in its wholeness.[4]

Within this ecclesial pattern, leaders of the Orthodox churches are honored and respected, but authority for teaching and transmitting the faith is believed to reside in the church as a whole and particularly in the wisdom of its bishops gathered in council. This is seen as the primary means of the Spirit's guidance of the church. Yet even so, as John Meyendorff notes, "A conciliar decree needed the 'reception' of the whole Church to be considered a true expression of the Tradition."[5] Here Scripture is viewed as authoritative *as part of the tradition,* not apart from it; and the ultimate authority in the transmission of the tradition is held to be the Spirit, no single bishop or patriarch.

This means that the forms of the church — its doctrines, rites, organization, and procedures — carry authority to the extent that they manifest and communicate the Spirit in the community of faith.[6] These forms serve to reflect the personality and activity of the Spirit within the divine Trinity and the cosmic activity of the Spirit as the giver and sustainer of life. Consequently, the liturgy is not confined within precise temporal limits but manifests the eternality of life that shares in or participates in the life of God.[7] Nor is spirituality confined only

---

4. See Kallistos Ware, *The Orthodox Way* (Crestwood, NY: St. Vladimir's Seminary Press, 1980); S. N. Bulgakov, *The Orthodox Church* (London: Centenary Press, 1935); and Nicolas Zernov, *Eastern Christendom* (New York: Putnam, 1961).

This and some of the following summaries draw upon research contributed by Dean Freiday, a representative of the Friends General Conference and a Sponsor of Catholic and Quaker studies, and an active member of the study group.

5. John Meyendorff, *Living Tradition* (Crestwood, NY: St. Vladimir's Seminary Press, 1978), 37.

6. Ibid., 15ff. and 30ff. See also Vladimir Lossky, *The Mystical Theology of the Eastern Church* (London: J. Clarke, 1957).

7. See, e.g., Alexander Schmemann, *Introduction to Liturgical Theology* (London: Faith Press, 1966).

to accepting and affirming certain beliefs, but has to do with the formation of the whole of life within the life of the church. This also indicates why the Orthodox church resists juridicalism in all its forms and insists that the structures of the church must prove their validity and authority through the actual exercise of their spiritual efficacy, that is to say, in their effective communication of the Spirit.

Orthodox churches maintain the offices of bishop, presbyter, and deacon, and ordain only men to these offices through the sacrament of Holy Orders. Patriarchs and Metropolitans govern the churches in their care by means of a permanent assembly of bishops called the Holy Synod. Parishes are administered by one or more councils *(ephory, epitrophy)*, of which the parish priest may be but is not necessarily a member. The priest is chosen sometimes by the *ephory,* and sometimes by the parishioners at large, but he has to be approved and appointed by the bishop. Decision-making is rendered through the synodical system with prayer and through invocation of the guidance of the Holy Spirit.

In essence, then, as Chrysostom Papadopoulis, Archbishop of Athens, has said, the church is to be seen as basically the organization and organism of the Spirit, both as visible and invisible. Its purpose is to draw people into union with Christ, and with God through Christ. The Spirit is here seen not as extraneous to the church's life through history and into eternity but as constituting the essence of its life. Hence, authority in the church is essentially spiritual and is to be exercised in ways that clearly manifest the Spirit.[8]

The Roman Catholic Church[9]

In Catholic ecclesiology the historical visible community of the faithful centered in and obedient to the bishop of Rome is seen as created by the Spirit, the same Spirit which also guides the church in its development through history as the body of Christ. The church is said to be the fruit of two divine missions, as Saint Thomas Aquinas put it: The Father, who is the principle without a beginning, sends the Son for the

---

8. As quoted in Donald Attwater, *The Christian Churches of the East,* Vol. 2 (London: Geoffrey Chapman, 1961), 144-45.

9. The following summary is drawn for the most part from a paper presented to the working group by Fr. Richard L. Foley.

salvation of the world. The Spirit who is also present in the world from the beginning is sent to communicate this salvation through the church and to draw humans into a new relation with God.[10] The church is seen, therefore, as the work of the Spirit in the whole of its life, in its ministry, worship, assemblies, works, and influence.

At the same time the Catholic church recognizes an ecclesial reality (or elements of such) in other Christian churches, but it believes that in its tradition the one church of Christ "subsists" in the sense that the essential reality and fullness of the church are presented in this tradition, even if not yet perfectly or fully manifested.[11] The church, as Vatican II affirmed, is *in via,* on the way to the goal of the coming of God's kingdom. On this journey the Spirit is active in the church in the development of its life and teaching and outreach to the world. This is evidenced most clearly in the classical marks of the church, in its unity, holiness, catholicity, and apostolicity.

Ultimately, it is the Holy Spirit that constitutes the essential unity of the church, the principle of communion that binds all the faithful together. The Spirit guides the formation and development of the church, working in and through its structure to create a unity of consent and of movement in the direction of God's calling. In this movement the Spirit works both through individuals and groups and through the magisterium to form its life in faithfulness to God's mission. In recent years there has been growing recognition that it is imperative that the church listen carefully and responsively to the cries of the poor and their yearning for freedom and life.[12] As it enters into solidarity with them the church may hear more clearly the Spirit's calling and empowerment.

The Holy Spirit is also seen as the principle of catholicity in the church, that which makes the church whole throughout the world. The church takes many varied forms in different cultures and local contexts, but running through all of these is a continuity of Spirit-inspired forms of identity — symbols, baptism, eucharist/mass, apos-

10. *Summa theologica* III: Q.1-59.

11. For more on this, see Francis A. Sullivan, S.J., *The Church We Believe In: One, Holy, Catholic and Apostolic* (New York: Paulist Press, 1988), chap. 2. The author contends that statements concerning the church in *Lumen gentium* must be understood in the light of the Decree on Ecumenism.

12. See, e.g., José I. González Faus, *Where the Spirit Breathes,* trans. Robert R. Barr (Maryknoll, NY: Orbis Books, 1989), esp. 105ff.

tolic mission, and so on. The Spirit makes the church catholic both in space, that is, throughout the world, and in time, through the centuries.

Furthermore, it is the Spirit that keeps the church apostolic, that is to say, in continuity with its origin in Jesus Christ and in the apostolic succession of its bishops through the ages. The Spirit-created and sustained apostolicity of the church is expressed also in its mission of witness and service. Indeed, the Spirit forms the church in a structure of ministry both to those within the church and those without.[13] Its life is to embody its servant Lord in service to the world. This to be demonstrated especially by those called to the sacrament of ministry within its life, in the service of its priests and bishops. They are to nurture and lead the people in their ministry as those whom God has invested by virtue of their office with a special power and authority to teach the faith and to guide the church. As Irenaeus said, "It is necessary to listen to the presbyters (bishops) who are in the church. They are the successors of the apostles and with the succession of the episcopate, they have received the certain charism of truth according to the good pleasure of the Father." The church teaches that through the episcopate the Spirit acts to teach and guide the church *ne finaliter erret,* so that error will not ultimately prevail (Matt. 15:18).

Finally, the Spirit is also the principle of the church's holiness. While the term "holy church" is not to be found as such in the New Testament, there are present similar expressions, such as "holy priesthood," "holy nation," and "holy temple." But the phrase does appear early in Christian tradition, for example, in Hippolytus: "Do you believe in the Holy Spirit in the holy church for the resurrection of the flesh?" The church is holy first of all because it is established and sanctified in Christ, but it is holy also because it is filled with the grace of the Holy Spirit who indwells the church (1 Cor. 3:16-17) and acts through it. Because this is so, the Spirit makes holy not only the church as a whole but also all of its members, whose lives in various ways (even if not unambiguously) manifest the holiness of the Spirit at work in them.

Certainly there are many questions under discussion these days about the forms of the church's life — issues concerning the priest-

---

13. A point that has been insightfully developed by Edward Schillebeeckx, *The Church with a Human Face: A New and Expanded Theology of Ministry* (New York: Crossroad, 1990), see esp. 115-23.

hood, moral and social stances of the church, disciplining of theolo-gians, and collegiality of bishops, to name only a few. But the church believes that it is and will be guided through these tumultuous times and in dealing with such issues by the same Spirit that has sustained and led the church through the centuries since its birth, the Spirit which gave it birth and which has nurtured its ongoing development.

The Lutheran Church[14]

The Lutheran Church, which grew out of the sixteenth-century Prot-estant Reformation in Germany and spread northward into the Scandi-navian countries — Greenland, North and South America — as well as to Africa, India, and other parts of the world, is for the most part synodical in structure. Yet this synodical form is expressed specifically in a variety of ethnic and regional patterns.[15] Holding Scripture to be normative, as interpreted according to the doctrinal statements col-lected in the *Book of Concord,* the church has nevertheless in the course of its history experienced a number of doctrinal and polity variations. On the North American church scene, the most prominent of these are the Lutheran Church–Missouri Synod and the recently formed Evangelical Lutheran Church in America. The latter was constituted by a merger in 1987 of The American Lutheran Church, The Lutheran Church in America, and The Association of Evangelical Lutheran Churches. In addition to these two major Lutheran bodies, there are also the Wisconsin Evangelical Lutheran Synod and several smaller bodies.[16]

Yet common to all Lutheran churches is the conviction that "justification by grace through faith" is at the heart of the gospel and that the whole life of the church is to bear witness to this. The Spirit

14. This statement was reviewed and revised by Prof. Winston Persaud, who teaches systematic theology at Wartburg Theological Seminary in Dubuque, Iowa; and by Dr. William Rusch, executive director of the office of ecumenical affairs for the Evangelical Lutheran Church in America.

15. See *The Lutheran Churches of the World,* ed. Alfred Th. Jorgensen et al. (Minneapolis: Augsburg, 1929-77). Also, Conrad John Immanuel Bergendorff, *The Church of the Lutheran Reformation* (St. Louis: Concordia Publishing House, 1967).

16. See E. Clifford Nelson, ed., *The Lutherans in North America* (Philadelphia: Fortress Press, 1975).

is understood as making effective and living in the church God's forgiveness of sins in Christ, which comes not through the law but through grace, and which the preaching of the word is constantly to hold before the church as that which is to guide the whole of the church's life and witness in and to the world.[17]

This is to be expressed and enacted also in the structures, polity, and decision-making of the church. These structures are generally regarded not as divinely prescribed but rather as practically determined, through the guidance of the Spirit, as expedient in different cultures and situations to serve the proclamation of the gospel.

In the Swedish Lutheran Church, episcopal organization has been maintained, but in most other Lutheran churches episcopacy has been replaced by a synodical structure. In some Lutheran churches a general synod embraces regional synods; while in others, such as the Missouri Synod, the synods maintain their independence. While there is considerable variety of church organization and procedures within the synods, most regional synods are comprised of an equal number of pastors and lay representatives, presided over by an elected president and a synod conference or convention. The general assembly or conference of synods is responsible for maintaining sound doctrine, governance of the church, and regulation of worship, as well as for missionary outreach. The Evangelical Lutheran Church in America is presided over by a bishop and other officers, convenes in churchwide assembly biennially to discuss and pass resolutions on matters before the church, and works through various divisions and commissions to implement decisions in the life of the church.

The Holy Spirit is perceived as working through or in conjunction with the word of God to guide and empower the church through these structures to respond faithfully to God's calling. Thus the structures, procedures, and decision-making of the church are to serve the proclamation of the gospel and are constantly tested by the Spirit as to the adequacy with which they do so. As Gritsch and Jenson point out, while the church is not simply to be identified with its institutional form, it creates organizational structures to carry out its

---

17. Cf. Regin Prenter, *Spiritus Creator*, trans. John M. Jensen (Philadelphia: Muhlenberg Press, 1953); also, Robert W. Jenson, "The Holy Spirit," and Philip J. Hefner, "The Church," in *Christian Dogmatics*, vol.2, ed. Carl E. Braaten and Robert W. Jenson (Philadelphia: Fortress Press, 1984).

mission.[18] In this way it seeks to follow the leading of the Spirit as the Spirit works through human historical judgment and organization. Not only is the Spirit discerned as working through present forms of the church but it is affirmed that the Spirit also engenders imagination and wisdom in the ongoing reorganization of the church to better serve in God's mission.

The Presbyterian Church

The recently united Presbyterian Church (U.S.A.), drawing on roots that reach back to John Calvin in Geneva and the Reformation in Scotland under the leadership of John Knox, and influenced also by the English Puritan Revolution and the Westminster Confession, professes Scripture as the sole ultimate rule of faith and practice for the church. However, from Calvin on, Word and Spirit have been closely conjoined in Reformed theology and tradition.[19] Scripture is considered basic and normative but its guidance can only be rightly heard and obeyed through the *testimonium spiritus sancti internum,* the inner witness of the Holy Spirit. And this is said to be as true for the church as a whole as it is for individual believers.[20]

The various Reformed confessions and catechisms attempt to summarize the biblical message and relate it to the contemporary situation but are subject to critical testing and restatement in the ongoing understanding of Scripture. This is held to be true also of the shaping of the church's life, its order, procedures, and specific ways of decision-making. The *Book of Order* begins with acknowledgment of Jesus Christ as the head of the church, whose presence in it causes its life to be christologically shaped. The constitution then proceeds to list a number of principles of church order, including the appointment of officers "not only to preach the gospel and administer the Sacraments but also to exercise discipline," and goes on to affirm that

18. Eric W. Gritsch and Robert W. Jenson, *Lutheranism: The Theological Movement and Its Confessional Writings* (Philadelphia: Fortress Press, 1976), 136.

19. See, e.g., John H. Leith, *An Introduction to the Reformed Tradition* (Atlanta: John Knox Press, 1977), 17-24.

20. E.g., Hendrikus Berkhof's remark: "The Word brings the Spirit to the heart, and the Spirit brings the Word within the heart." *The Doctrine of the Holy Spirit* (Richmond, VA: John Knox Press, 1964), 38.

all church power is "only ministerial and declarative" and valid only insofar as consistent with Scripture and conscience.[21]

John Leith has said that "presbyterianism is not a fixed pattern of church life but a developing pattern that has both continuity and diversity."[22] It takes somewhat different forms in Scotland, in America, and elsewhere in the world. In America it has developed a representative system from the presbytery to the synod to the general assembly. A key element in this structure is the ruling or teaching elder as representative of the people, although there are differences among Presbyterians as to whether this office is to be seen as more lay or clerical in nature.[23] Such elders participate, for instance, in the ordination of ministers; they may also preach and teach; and together with the clergy they "exercise leadership, government, and discipline" in the church "and have responsibilities for the life of a particular church as well as the church-at-large, including ecumenical relationships."[24]

Increasingly, though, it is being recognized that even this locally based form of church governance can be culturally biased and discriminatory, and committees on representation are called for to ensure a more truly representative presence of women and men and racial and ethnic minorities on all the governing councils of the church.[25] There is also growing concern that decision-making in the church include persons from those groups and segments of society which have tended to be ignored, such as the handicapped, Asian-Americans, and Amerindians.[26]

This is important because it is believed that ultimately it is the Spirit working in and through such representative councils that exercises true authority in the church and that is a constantly creative force in the church's life. More particularly, the Spirit is said to generate continuing reform and renewal in the life of the church; it makes the church an *ecclesia reformada et semper reformanda*, reformed and always in the process of being reformed.

21. *The Constitution of the Presbyterian Church (U.S.A.), Part II: Book of Order* (Louisville, KY: Office of the General Assembly, 1981, 1988), G-9.

22. Leith, *An Introduction to the Reformed Tradition*, 147.

23. Ibid., 153.

24. *Book of Order*, G-6.0300.

25. *Book of Order*, G-9.0105.

26. Instrumental in raising consciousness and responsiveness to marginalized segments of the church has been the Commission on Ecumenical Mission and Relations (COEMAR). See Donald Black, *Merging Mission and Unity* (Philadelphia: Geneva Press, 1986).

African Methodist Episcopal Zion Church[27]

The African Methodist Episcopal Zion Church is an integral part of the Wesleyan Methodist tradition of the Protestant faith. In conjunction with the rest of Methodism, the A.M.E. Zion Church believes that the "Church is present wherever the pure word of God is preached and the Holy Sacraments are duly administered. It is the communion and fellowship of all believers, and Jesus Christ is its Redeemer and Lord." Though comprised of mortal human beings, it is nevertheless believed to be the "body of Christ in which his Holy Spirit is incarnate, welding all its members into the society of God." The church is not regarded as itself the kingdom of God, but rather as the corporate instrument through which humans and God are working together to perfect the reign of God in individual life and social relations.[28]

The Holy Spirit is vital to the individual Christian life and to the church. The Spirit floods the life of the believer and guides and strengthens her or him in a new way of life. God through Christ has made the Holy Spirit available to all people, and those who trust in Christ will receive and invariably become transformed by the Spirit.[29] The Spirit is believed to be operative in every function of the church, continuing from its worship into its forms and structures.

Methodists insist that a conscious experience of the love and grace of God in worship engenders religious enthusiasm — in preaching, praying, singing, and living. A Methodist Christian feels himself or herself lifted up, fired up with an unusual, transcendent experience, the motive of which is love. The witness of the Holy Spirit assures God's love for the worshipers and elicits from them a joyful and enthusiastic response of love.[30] As a response of thanksgiving for God's holy love revealed supremely in Jesus Christ, A.M.E. Zionists are enabled to join those who in all times and places have offered the sacrifice of praise and obedience to God through Christ, who through

---

27. The following summary was contributed by pastor and professor Dr. Mozella G. Mitchell, who teaches in the Department of Religious Studies of the University of South Florida and is pastor of the A.M.E. Zion Church in Brandon.

28. A.M.E. Zion Church, *Know Your Church*, 3rd ed. (Charlotte, N.C.: The A.M.E. Zion Publishing House, 1953), 7-9.

29. Ibid., 8, 10.

30. Ibid., 28.

his supreme sacrifice is our intercessor with God. Christ joins us to himself in worship by the renewing power of the Holy Spirit.[31]

According to the official statement of the church, "corporate worship centers in the proclamation of the Word and the celebration of the Sacraments. The individual believer's prayer, obedience, and service are essential components for the entire community's worship."[32] The worshiping community offers itself to God in common acts of praise, confession of sin, thanksgiving, prayer, reading and hearing of the Word of God, affirmation of faith, and celebration of the sacraments. The lively participation of all members in worship is realized through singing, preaching, hearing, and response. The activity of the Holy Spirit is recognized and acknowledged in the leaders of worship and in the individual worshipers, as well as in the unified body of worshipers. The Spirit enters the gathering community at the opening of worship and is invoked through the call to worship and prayer. Sharing in the Spirit is a process that continues throughout the worship service. And at the close of the service the Spirit guides the communicants into works of service and social and spiritual commitment in the world, where the Spirit is also constantly at work building, encouraging, inspiring, unifying, and empowering people in the work of God.

The Spirit which is active and manifested in worship does not cease to influence communicants and church leaders in group meetings and business and administrative sessions, which are held either immediately following worship or even later in the week. For to a significant degree, Spirit-guided leadership is expected and sought in all matters concerning the church.

As to the Spirit's role in the structures, governance, discipline, authority, and decision-making in the A.M.E. Zion Church, it is believed and affirmed that the Holy Spirit inspires and guides these processes. The hierarchy of episcopal government consists of bishops, presiding elders, pastors, deacons, local preachers, and lay officers and members. No one individual is the absolute authority in the church. But corporate structures in which all participate at some level are the governing authority of the church through which the workings of the

---

31. *The Quadrennial Episcopal Address of the Board of Bishops to the Forty-Second Session of the General Conference of the African Methodist Episcopal Zion Church.* St. Louis, Missouri, July 25–August 3, 1984, 6-7.

32. Ibid., 7.

Holy Spirit are made evident. The General Conference, held quadrennially, is the highest law-making and governing agency of the church. It is composed of equal numbers of ministerial and lay delegates from all annual conferences of the church. Each episcopal district is presided over by a bishop and consists of a number of annual conferences, each with districts presided over by elders who serve and oversee the district churches under the authority and direction of the presiding bishop. Pastors of individual churches receive their charges from the bishop under the careful guidance of the Spirit and are expected to serve in accordance with the *Discipline* of the A.M.E. Zion Church and the leading of the Spirit. The people recognize the guidance of the Spirit in these forms and structures, but all are aware that human imperfections and the possibilities and occurrences of error and weaknesses can also manifest themselves in these, and they make allowances for such.

The Church of God (Anderson, Indiana)[33]

The Church of God practices what historically it has called charismatic church government. Emphasizing that the basis of the church's life is a personal relation to God and Christ through Scripture experienced in a definite act of conversion and salvation,[34] the movement has insisted that it is this alone that makes one a member of the church, rather than any formal rite. Corresponding to this is a view of church government which holds that God is the ultimate governing authority in the life of the church, and thus ecclesiastical position does not in and of itself constitute final authority. Only to the degree that those in ecclesiastical positions are perceived by the fellowship of believers to be functioning in harmony with the fellowship's understanding of the will of Christ revealed in Scripture by the Spirit do they exercise authority. Their authority is thus only that of "spiritual and moral suasion."

33. The following summary is drawn largely from a paper presented to the study group by Gilbert W. Stafford, professor at the Anderson University School of Theology, Anderson, Indiana.

34. See D. S. Warner, *Salvation: Present, Perfect, Now or Never* (Moundsville, WV: Gospel Trumpet, n.d.); also, Frederick George Smith, *What the Bible Teaches: A Systematic Presentation of the Fundamental Principles of Biblical Truth* (Anderson, IN: Gospel Trumpet, 1955).

Congregations are autonomous and self-governing and call their own pastors. Pastors are, however, ordained by a council of ministers at state or regional assemblies. But such persons are not endowed by the church with any special power and authority; rather, they are *recognized* as having been called, anointed, and sent by God to serve and lead the church. It is the church's responsibility in the power of the Holy Spirit to recognize God's hand in this and to bless those who have been sent by God.[35]

More specifically in terms of church organization and processes of decision-making, this results in a wide variety of patterns both among local congregations and in regional structures.[36] It also results in the absence of any regional, national, or international body or officer with the power to speak and act authoritatively for the church. In the local congregation, the pastor serves as a spiritual guide and leader but works with a board of deacons or councilors to make decisions, which are then submitted to the congregation as a whole for confirmation by vote. The church's officers and councils therefore exercise authority only to the extent that their decisions and actions are perceived and accepted by the people as truly in line with Scripture and recognized as inspired by the Spirit.

When such church organization functions as it should, it includes several key components. Among these are that (1) power is exercised along horizontal, egalitarian rather than vertical, hierarchical lines; (2) such power is clearly grounded in Scripture and in a personal relationship to Christ and God; (3) power and authority in the church are exercised through relationships of spiritual and moral suasion, not domination and coercion; (4) the exercise of such power is unitive and upbuilds the community in love and life in Christ, rather than being divisive; (5) it allows for ongoing responsiveness to the leading of the Holy Spirit; and (6) it gives priority in the governance of the church to preaching and teaching the faith rather than to techniques of administration and management.

35. See John W. Smith, *Heralds of a Brighter Day* (Anderson, IN: Gospel Trumpet, 1955).

36. See Charles Ewing Brown, *When the Trumpet Sounded: A History of the Church of God Movement* (Anderson, IN: Warner Press, 1951).

Some Observations and Reflections

On the basis of this brief survey of some forms of church organization and the ways in which the Spirit is perceived as active in and through them,[37] what can we say concerning the work of the Spirit in the formation and forms of the church? (The following comments express more the views of the authors of this chapter than a consensus statement of our study group, although these reflections were discussed in the group.)

Surely one thing that becomes obvious at once is that the Spirit seems to delight in variety! As we have listened to one another relate how the Spirit is experienced at work in the patterns of our various church traditions, we have come to appreciate more deeply that, running through all the human factors involved, it is clear that the Spirit has been at work in the formation of these various church traditions. It seems that the Spirit moves and works through a wide variety of forms of church life to bring salvation and to meet the various needs of people.

At the same time we recognize in this amazing variety that it is nevertheless one and the same Spirit who is at work. The Spirit does give a variety of gifts but, as the apostle points out, it is "the same Spirit" who is active in this "variety of workings" and "who inspires them all in every one" (1 Cor. 12:4ff.). Moreover, it is only through the enlightenment given by this same Spirit that we are led to recognize more clearly and fully that it is indeed the one Spirit who is at work in this variety of church forms. But far from this making us comfortable with our present dividedness and virtual isolation as churches, such recognition creates a desire to learn more of what the Spirit has to teach us through other church traditions as well as our own. Indeed, it has been precisely through the process of learning more of the work of the Spirit in traditions other than our own that we have come to see and understand the work of the Spirit in our own traditions more fully.

But we must also say more. To recognize that the Spirit is involved in shaping and working in and through the various church

37. In addition to those included here, the study group also considered papers and studies of the Churches of Christ, the Christian Church (Disciples of Christ), Assemblies of God, Society of Friends, United Church of Christ, Metropolitan Community Churches, Episcopalian, and Swedenborgian church traditions.

traditions raises even more acutely the question of how to discern where and to what extent the Spirit is at work in these various forms of church life and in their decision-making and implementing procedures, and to what extent fallible and sometimes misguided human desires and calculations are determinative here. Are there any criteria that can be of assistance in making such distinctions? It seems to us that certainly one such criterion, and perhaps the key one, is that which Jesus set forth when he instructed his disciples, "The kings of the Gentiles lord it over them; and those in authority over them are called benefactors. But not so with you; rather the greatest among you must become like the youngest; and the leader like one who serves" (Luke 22:25-26, NRSV). If the Spirit at work in the church is the Spirit who comes through this one, who is himself among us as "one who serves" (Luke 22:27), then surely we must say that the Spirit works to create patterns and structures of church life that, in all their variety, are forms of service and witness.

The ideal therefore that the Spirit generates in the churches to guide their life is that of *agapē* — of love and respect and humility and unity in Christ's mission. This means not only that love is to be the formative principle of church order, but that the ordering and order of the church must seek to express more clearly that it is of the very essence of this community to be a community of love demonstrated in justice-seeking, precisely because it is graced and guided by the Spirit of the just and loving God.

Surely another criterion of the activity of the Spirit in the formation and forms of the church's life is whether and to what extent these forms manifest a "hunger and thirst for righteousness" (Matt. 5:6). If the church lives in the movement of the Spirit that is working unceasingly to mend and transform creation, then the forms of its own life must conduce to such healing. To put it negatively, forms that separate and alienate people from one another and from the rest of creation resist the Spirit's movement. (Is this also at least part of what is meant by the perplexing statement about "blasphemy against the Holy Spirit" [Mark 3:29-30]?) But to put the matter positively, those forms and reforms of the church's life which contribute to breaking down barriers, overcoming injustice, and reconciling people can serve the Spirit in its work to make the creation well.

Consequently, it can never be said of the order of the church that it is an end in itself. Its validity and authority are essentially and ultimately spiritual in character. There may be times and circumstances in which church members must render obedience to church structures and directives even though they do not understand clearly the biblical and spiritual grounds underlying these. But this can only be exceptional and temporary, never the normal use of power and authority in the church. For obedience in faith must finally be in accord with conscience, and thus the recognition that the directive of the church — whether it comes from the pope, or from a church council, or from an individual who claims to have been moved by the Spirit, or from a vote of a congregation — is truly in accord with God's will and mission. For it is as true within the church as it is in relation to authorities outside it that finally "we must obey God" (Acts 5:29, 39).

There is, to be sure, always some degree of ambiguity in the decisions and actions of the church, since human wisdom is always limited and every decision and action is inevitably affected by a mixture of motives. To recognize that this is so is not, however, to deny that the Spirit acts in and through such decisions and actions, judging their limitations and elements of infidelity but also often using them to guide the church in God's service. The Spirit is not afraid to get involved in and to work concretely through the nitty-gritty of human decision-making and implementation![38] Also, the Spirit works in and through the church to lead it in reviewing and evaluating its structures and procedures. Such evaluation is not unambiguous, of course, but it can serve as an instrument of the Spirit in correcting abuses and in striving for greater faithfulness in the church. Even more, it can serve as a means of the Spirit's making the church a more effective agent in responding to the cries of those hurting and in need around the world today.

The order of the church, then, must be ultimately and ideally an order of service and witness. It must be an order that leads to justice, that is, to forming human life in ways that conduce to the well-being of all. Such justice has both retributive and distributive aspects. It involves discipline and clear lines of responsibility and accountability; that is its retributive dimension. But its distributive aspect is even more

---

38. See Arnold B. Come, *Human Spirit and Holy Spirit* (Philadelphia: Westminster Press, 1959); José Comblin, *The Holy Spirit and Liberation* (Maryknoll, NY: Orbis Books, 1989); and Yves Congar, *Called to Life* (New York: Crossroad, 1987).

important, namely, in its use of its resources — including people, finances, heritage, and influence — to bear faithful witness to the gospel. One of the clearest manifestations of the Spirit moving in the life of the church is when the church uses its resources to be a source for healing and transformation of the world.

But in carrying out this mission the church always seems to be beset by two temptations. On the one hand, it is tempted to claim for itself and its forms the authority that properly belongs ultimately only to God. On the other hand, some may also be tempted at times to despair of the church and its inherited structures and to rebel against them, leading to further division within the church. Even movements which do not set out to divide the church but to reform it often produce churches alienated from the others, thus contributing to the further fracturing of the body of Christ. Frequently in such instances there are manifested anti-authoritarian human tendencies and assertions of individualism and egotism, as is evident in many of the church conflicts in America, as elsewhere. Disobedience and rebellion cannot, however, be summarily condemned in all cases, as the civil rights movement, for example, makes clear. But such movements require a careful discernment of the spirits, which is also of course just as true of movements favoring conservatism and hesitancy to change. In movements of protest and reform, there may be a large amount of uncertainty as to just where the Spirit is leading, but that does not necessarily mean that the Spirit is absent nor completely hidden in such movements. The criteria for discerning the Spirit's work which we have discussed earlier can be helpful here. We might also ask, To what extent do such movements manifest compassion and protection of life, and thus evidence the Spirit who is the giver and nourisher of life?

It seems to be true that all organizations have their rise, their peak of fullest development, and their period of decline.[39] Is this also true of the church and its structures? Scripture records the promise of the risen Christ to be with the church "to the close of the age" (Matt. 28:20; 16:18; Eph. 1:4-10). At the same time Scripture also reminds the church that it cannot take Christ's presence and the activity of the

---

39. This has been investigated in great detail by the great Harvard sociologist P. Sorokin in his work *Society, Culture and Personality* (New York: Cooper Square, 1962).

Spirit within it for granted (1 Pet. 4:17; Rev. 2–3). The Jesus movement was initially a reform movement within Judaism. Many of Jesus' pronouncements point out critically that even within his own faith community at the time, human regulations were being given precedence over divine direction. But even so, Jesus did not dissociate himself from his religious tradition nor reject its structure wholesale. Rather, he called for faithfulness to the "weightier matters of the law" and to the Spirit which inspired them (Matt. 23:23). When this is also the church's primary concern it will not need to be preoccupied about matters of survival or the attractiveness of its "image," but it will demonstrate in the vitality of its life and vision — and in the forms of its life — that it lives in the power of the Spirit of the eternal God.

Yet such vitality will involve wrestling with many difficult issues in contemporary church life and the church's relation to the world. Should, for instance, the church ordain professed and practicing gay and lesbian persons into the ministry? Should the church support or oppose abortion, and for what reasons; and should it see unlawful actions against abortion clinics as justified, or not, even when this proceeds from strong religious convictions? Should the church support state funding of programs of religious education, and if so, under what conditions? Should there be censure of those churches and congregations which discriminate on the basis of race or sex or social or economic status? A church that is alive in the Spirit will not avoid such issues but will address and struggle with them in a spirit of love and respect that affirms those who disagree and yet endeavors to witness to the truth while maintaining the unity of the Spirit (see Eph. 2:19-22). Admittedly, that is not easy; it requires a great deal of patience and understanding, and willingness to listen and learn as well as to speak out and instruct. Yet the Spirit is not just a reinforcer of ideas and dispositions that we are "comfortable with," but rather the Spirit at work in the church is the Spirit of the God who is always much greater than we have conceived and can imagine. This Spirit can at times "take sides," but more often it works through an exchange of views, the interaction of give-and-take, a process of mutual learning and correction in which the church is led, albeit sometimes stumblingly, toward God's calling. Certainly there are some decisions that cannot wait for long debate and interminable "study," and where those in positions to do so must take the risk of speaking and acting for the church. But such actions are always subject to testing in the ongoing work of the Spirit. One aspect of such testing is the extent to which these decisions and actions serve the general and greatest good. But ultimately the test is whether they lead the church to be faithful to its calling. Every church order and procedure of decision-making is judged finally by the Spirit of truth (John 14:17) that comes from above and works to lead the church to do what is right.

Chapter Six

Spirit and Ministry

RENA M. YOCOM

Through the Holy Spirit the church continues the revelation of God in Christ across the face of the earth by joining God in a mission. By . . . the power of the Holy Spirit, the church joins God's mission to reclaim, restore and redeem the life of all creation to its God-intended design.[1]

Rarely does the church debate whether or not we should be in mission and ministry. But regularly the church does debate and becomes divided when we consider which ecclesiologies God can best use for such sacred tasks. The forms for accomplishing our work may vary, yet most agree that ministry is not only the responsibility of the whole church, it is also the call of each one within the corporate body of Christ.

The Spirit Bestows Gifts

Now there are varieties of gifts, but the same Spirit; and there are varieties of service, but the same Lord. . . . To each is given

1. "Partnership in God's Mission" (New York: General Board of Global Ministries, United Methodist Church, 1990).

Rena M. Yocom, a diaconal minister (permanent deacon), is the Associate General Secretary of the Mission Education and Cultivation Program department of the General Board of Global Ministries of The United Methodist Church.

the manifestation of the Spirit for the common good. (1 Cor. 12:4-7)

These words of Paul are restated and affirmed by the ecumenical community both in *Baptism, Eucharist, Ministry* and in *Confessing One Faith:*

The Holy Spirit bestows on the community diverse and complimentary gifts. These are for the common good of the whole people and are manifested in acts of service within the community and to the world.[2]

All members are called to discover, with the help of the community, the gifts they have received and to use them for the building up of the Church and for service of the world to which the Church is sent.[3]

The Spirit pours out an abundance of charisms. These charisms are for the building up of the church and for service in the world through teaching, prophecy, healing, miracles, tongues and discernment of spirits.[4]

All Christian ministry is defined and characterized by Christ's selfless and self-giving life. The Spirit calls and empowers all Christians into this ministry of the risen Christ. Although there is only one ministry, there are many forms. There is one Christ, yet there are diverse gifts within the one body of Christ (Eph. 4:4-16).

The word *charism* refers to the gifts which are understood to be God-given. As BEM states, "The word *charism* denotes the gifts bestowed by the Holy Spirit on any member of the body of Christ for the building up of the community and the fulfillment of its calling."[5]

Some churches understand charisms to be given at baptism. Some specifically connect charism with chrismation (the anointing with oil). Others would distinguish between the ordinary gifts or fruits of the Spirit, such as love, faith, generosity, and self-control, which belong

2. *Baptism, Eucharist, Ministry,* Faith and Order Paper No. 111 (Geneva: World Council of Churches, 1982), sec. on "Ministry," par. 5, p. 20.

3. Ibid.

4. *Confessing One Faith,* Faith and Order Paper No. 140 (Geneva: World Council of Churches, 1987), 187.

5. BEM, par. 7a, p. 21.

to all, and the extraordinary gifts of the Spirit, such as healing and speaking in tongues, which belong to a few. These extraordinary gifts may belong to lay and clergy alike. Some churches hold that there is a special gifting of the Spirit bestowed in the act of ordination.

The Spirit Calls and the Spirit Enables Discernment

H. Richard Niebuhr, in his now classic book *The Purpose of the Church and Its Ministry,* articulates four senses of the calling to ministry:

1. The call to be a Christian, which is variously described as the call to discipleship of Jesus Christ, to hearing and doing of the Word of God, to repentance and faith;
2. The secret call, namely, that inner persuasion or experience whereby a person feels directly summoned or invited by God to take up the work of the full-time ministry;
3. The providential call, which is that invitation to assume the work of full-time ministry which comes through the equipment of a person with the gifts for the exercise of such ministry and/or through the divine guidance of one's life by all its circumstances;
4. The ecclesiastical call, that is, the summons and invitation extended . . . by some community or institution of the church to engage in the work of the full-time or ordained ministry.[6]

1. The Call To Be Christian

There has never been a time in which the first calling, the call to be Christian, was not assumed as the necessary first step for all ministry. When the U.S. churches responded to BEM, the clearest consensus was that ministry begins with the calling and serving of the whole people of God.[7] There might have been more agreement in the rest of the ministry section of BEM if this beginning had not been overshadowed as the discussion turned to the matter of ordination.

6. H. Richard Niebuhr, *The Purpose of the Church and Its Ministry* (New York: Harper & Row, 1956), 64.
7. Rena M. Yocom, "Synthesis of Responses Regarding Ministry," *American Baptist Quarterly* 7 (March 1988).

Jack Carroll points out that when this larger base for defining ministry is not present, "laity become, at best, a supporting cast and, at worst, the audience that is entertained and edified by the star — the 'real' minister. And, of course, if they do not like the performance, they can always hire a new lead actor."[8]

Religion in the United States, as well as the culture at large, contains a healthy dose of egalitarianism. This is usually expressed theologically in the doctrine of the priesthood of all believers. Yet within this egalitarianism there are a number of ways of conceiving what this means specifically up to and including the idea that "ordained persons are nice but not needed." In fact, American-born churches use ordination in very limited circumstances.

In the last three decades there has been a resurgence of emphasis on the ministry of all members of the church. For Catholics, this new emphasis was accelerated by the Second Vatican Council. For Protestants, there have been two renewing influential movements. One, surfacing in the nomenclature of the day, was referred to as "lay empowerment" or the "grass roots" movement. The second was the rise in feminist leadership with its strong emphasis on partnership and mutuality in ministry and a resistance to patterns of hierarchy and domination. This developing theological understanding of the general ministry of the church has now been reinforced through the structural organization of most denominations, with many conferences, assemblies, and boards requiring an equal number of lay and ordained participants.

2. The Secret Call

The understanding that God has called and that the Spirit has empowered certain persons to preach and lead others is very ancient. Sometimes these persons were the ones who held official ecclesial position; sometimes they were not.

There are many biblical accounts of God's calling. We can recall not only Samuel, Isaiah, and Amos but also Rahab, Shiprah, and Puah as individuals called by God. Jesus called specific persons such as Peter and Andrew and Mary, the Magdalene. And how would the early

8. Jackson Carroll, *As One with Authority* (Louisville: John Knox Press, 1991), 88.

church have taken shape without the call and response of Paul, Stephen, Lydia, Priscilla, and Aquila? There is a whole litany of names of persons who, upon hearing God's secret call, moved forward to lead the church.

During the Reformation, John Calvin wrote that "no one should assume public office in the Church without being called." Calvin realized that this call consisted of two parts, both an inner and an outer experience. But Calvin's concern for order as well as ardor led him to write more about the outward call and the process of election.[9]

John Wesley, on the other hand, built a needed ministry of renewal using lay preachers who had no "ecclesiastical call" from the church. In a sermon entitled "A Caution Against Bigotry," he said, "I allow that it is highly expedient, whoever preaches in His name should have an outward as well as inward call; but that it is absolutely necessary, I deny."[10] When Wesley adapted the Articles of Religion for the Methodists, he omitted Number 23 which referred to the *rite vocatus,* the "lawfully called," who in the Anglican church alone had the right to the office of public preaching and ministering the sacraments in the congregation. Wesley wrote an explanatory note concerning this in his *Letters:*

> I apprehend indeed that there ought, if possible, to be both an outward and inward call to this work; yet, if one of the two be supposed wanting [lacking], I had rather want [lack] the outward than the inward call. I rejoice that I am called to preach the Gospel both by God and man. Yet I acknowledge, I had rather have the divine without the human, than the human without the divine call.[11]

Evangelical Protestants in this country (which, Jack Carroll reminds us, constituted the majority of Protestants in the nineteenth century)

9. Robert Henderson, "The Ministry in Word and Sacrament," in *Ordination: Past, Present, Future,* ed. Jack Rogers and Deborah Mullen (Louisville: Presbyterian Publishing House, 1990), 97.

10. John Wesley, cited in III.6, "United Methodist Response — Baptism, Eucharist and Ministry," TMs [photocopy] Task Force appointed by General Commission on Christian Unity and Interreligious Concerns and the Council of Bishops.

11. John Wesley, *Letters,* III, 195, as cited by Franz Hildebrandt in his essay "The Meaning of Ordination in Methodism" (Nashville: Department of Ministerial Education, Board of Education, 1960), 68.

have always given a greater emphasis to the inward call than to a sacramental, ecclesial one. Yet an inward call is never solely sufficient. It must bear some outward sign, identification, and accountability.

3. The Providential Call

Many persons have written about the call to ministry in a bifurcated way, sharply dividing inner and outer, private and public, individual and communal aspects. In Niebuhr's typology, however, there is the providential call and experience which is more evident than the secret call, yet is something other than the full ecclesiastically authorized sacramental ministry. Niebuhr saw this as one component of the total call to ministry, either following or preceding the secret call.

However, there may be examples of this category in which one has assumed the work of full-time ministry before the church has recognized a particular calling as fully valid. One example of this is the lay preacher of the Wesleyan tradition which was mentioned earlier. Another more current illustration which reaches across many denominational lines is that of the diaconal ministry.

One of the most debated issues in the plethora of ministry studies today is the office of deacon. The traditional role of deacon has been found to be too limited; that is, all too often the function of such persons is only to assist in the liturgy: they "have ceased to fulfill any function with regard to the diaconal witness of the Church."[12] Those in the ground swell of renewal want a deacon's office that is, perhaps, truer to the definition of the word and more explicitly representative of Christ's call to serve, as indicated in *The COCU Consensus:*

> It is a ministry in its own right and not a stepping-stone to other offices. . . . It is neither "special," marginal, supplementary, nor compensatory.[13]

Yet denominations, communions, and ecumenical bodies are all equally unsure about the appropriate form for this revitalized diaconate. Compare, for instance, this statement:

12. Gerald Moede, ed., *The COCU Consensus* (Princeton: Consultation on Christian Union, 1985), par. 43, p. 48.
13. Ibid., par. 62, p. 53.

To undertake this work of restoration and reformation will require serious research, imaginative thought, and mutual consultation. This document [the *COCU Consensus*] cannot, therefore, specify ahead of time the exact form of a restored diaconate, or delineate the changes and reforms that a revitalization of the diaconate would entail for the churches.[14]

Edward Schillebeeckx suggests two alternatives for resolution. One possibility is to give "a completely new content" to the ministry of deacon; the second is to create a fourth ministry (to accompany the traditional threefold pattern) which would include the laying on of hands with an invocation *(epiclesis)* in "a prayer in which the task . . . is precisely described" in a particular situation.[15]

Actually, both avenues are currently being used, though there is no consensus about either. The permanent ordained deacon in the Orthodox tradition fulfills a primarily liturgical role, while the lay deacon in the Baptist tradition fills primarily a governance role. Both the Catholic and the Episcopal traditions have a transitional and a permanent diaconate, while the United Methodists have a unique term: "diaconal minister." The Methodist Church of New Zealand, the United Church of Australia, and the United Church of Canada have adopted the type of permanent deacon that has been described in recent ecumenical documents.

Yet even while committees meet and debate, and groups take stands and conferences vote, there are individuals, called both secretly and providentially, who are already participants in the full-time public diaconal ministry of the church of Jesus Christ.

4. The Ecclesiastical Call

Ordination is frequently referred to as a "rite of the church." Defining ordination in this way puts primary emphasis on the ecclesiastical call. The ordinand has met certain qualifications or testing so that the community is assured of the needed gifts, talents, and motivation that will enable this person who is called to function in a representative ministry. BEM articulates this role in this way:

14. Ibid., par. 61, p. 53.
15. Edward Schillebeeckx, *The Church with a Human Face* (New York: Crossroad, 1988), 266.

There is a personal awareness of a call from the Lord to dedicate oneself to the ordained ministry. This call may be discerned through personal prayer and reflection. . . . This call must be authenticated by the Church's recognition of the gifts and graces of the particular person, both natural and spiritually given, needed for the ministry to be performed.[16]

Traditionally in some denominations, such as the Church of the Brethren, the congregation elects persons into pastoral ministry. In this view, ministry belongs to the whole people of God; therefore calling to ministry belongs to the whole people.[17] This community call often precedes and/or prompts the inner call. If there is no inner sense of calling, there will of course be no affirmative response to the congregation's call. When culture emphasizes individualism, as ours does, it is the responsibility of the individual to discern the call and then test this possibility through the church's representative structures.

The clergy role or office contains normative expectations about what it means to be representatives of the sacred. Jack Carroll explains, "Though they vary by denominational tradition and local culture, these expectations are built into the role."[18] Thus the office itself acts as a continuing guide, regardless of the subjective state of the individual.

Marianne Wolfe describes the ecclesiastical call in a personal way as "an invitation" to use the gifts that have been given the person. "We have all had the experience of recognizing within ourselves a call to use a particular gift. . . . [But] our private, inner call must be validated by the public call in which our gift is recognized by others who choose us to fulfill a particular work. A doctor cannot serve until chosen by a patient; a lawyer, by a client. . . ."[19]

Niebuhr understood all four calls to be elements of one phenomenon. They are distinguishable yet not separable, and are equal in importance. A disproportionate emphasis given any one of these calls will produce a distortion both in the process and preparation for

16. BEM, par. 45, p. 31.
17. Don Miller, "Study of Ministry: Church of the Brethren," TMs (New York: Faith and Order Commission, 1990), 3
18. Carroll, *As One with Authority,* 199.
19. Marianne Wolfe, "The Elder Ministry in the Presbyterian Church (U.S.A.)," in *Ordination: Past, Present, and Future,* 59.

ministry. If total emphasis were placed on the "secret call," and certain persons of questionable integrity declared that they were called by God, who could question or intercede on the community's behalf? Such self-declared untested calling can, and has in history, led to situations that were harmful to the church and its mission.

When the base criteria for entering ministry (and perhaps full membership into a ministerial conference) is a master's degree, there is a risk that academic aptitude would become the only legitimate sign of God's Spirit and call. When the ecclesiastical call looms predominant, problems can surface around an "applicant/employer" mentality. When gifted persons, trained and serving the church in some way, are prevented by the "system" from using these gifts because of vocation, gender, marital status, or educational level, there emerge inevitably both frustration and anger. Even worse, the church becomes ineffective as Christ's witness to the world.

For ministry in the body of Christ, it is God who calls, the individual who responds, and the community that discerns, authenticates, and authorizes that ministry. The Spirit is not bound by the church, yet in gracious response to the church's invocation, the Spirit affirms, increases, and strengthens the *charisms* on which the ecclesiastical call is based.

Ordination/Epiclesis

Through the Holy Spirit, God in Christ empowers ministry and sends the church into the world. The Spirit convicts, convinces, and comforts, bestowing both the gifts for ministry and the enabling grace by which these gifts are discerned, claimed, and utilized.

Since the origination of the church described in the New Testament, certain individual Christians have preached and taught, exercised oversight, and led in worship. The election of these individuals and their gifts was called "ordering for ministry." BEM states, "As Christ chose and sent apostles, Christ continues through the Holy Spirit to choose and call persons into the ordained ministry."[20] Ordination, like baptism, is a gift of the Spirit of God at work in the community of faith. Yet unlike baptism, which is offered to all the faithful, ordi-

20. BEM, par. 11, p. 21.

nation is for those baptized in whom the church discerns particular gifts for leadership and representative ministry.

Ordination symbolizes the ecclesiastical call in response to the divine call. The verbal calling by name makes the occasion very personal as well as communal. The Spirit works within and through this rite of entry into representative ministry to effect a new relationship, a new reality.

BEM defines ordination by "the laying on of hands of those appointed to do so [which] is at one and the same time invocation of the Holy Spirit *(epiklesis);* sacramental sign; acknowledgement of gifts and commitment."[21] Although some traditions may more readily associate *epiclesis* with the eucharist rather than ordination, *epiclesis* is the invocation or the specific petition for the special in-flowing of the active power of God. The most traditional, and at one time mandatory, form of this invocation is the *Veni, Creator Spiritus:*

> Come, O Creator Spirit, come,
> And make within our hearts thy home;
> To us thy grace celestial give,
> Who of thy breathing move and live.
>
> O Paraclete, that name is thine
> Of God most high the gift divine;
> The well of life, the fire of love,
> Our soul's anointing from above. . . .

The ordination prayer or invocation asks for the gift of God's continuing power upon and within the ordinand for the exercise of a particular ministry. By praying that the ordinand may receive God's Spirit, the church acknowledges God's initiative and power and the church's continual dependence on God to bless its ministry. Since ordination is essentially a setting apart with prayer for the gift of the Holy Spirit, the authority of the ordained ministry is not to be understood as the possession of the ordained person but as a gift for the continuing edification of the whole body of the church.

There has never been unanimity on either the nomenclature or the concepts undergirding ordination. In secular Rome, a distinction was drawn between the *ordo* (the senate) and the *plebeians* or *populus*

---

21. Ibid., par. 41, p. 30.

romanus. This secular distinction in dignity was later transferred into the church and the language of *ordo* was used for clergy as well. Clergy began wearing distinctive garb that corresponded to that of superior ranks in society.

However, in the Greek culture, the word *cheirotonein* was used for clergy. This meant something akin to "appointment" or "designation." Thus, in the New Testament there is simply an appointment recorded, followed by the laying on of hands and prayer for the Spirit. Those traditions which emphasize the Greek heritage will therefore speak more about functions which the ordained assume on behalf of the faith community.

It may be that in recent discussion of representative ministry, we have in the making a paradigm shift from both of the two views mentioned above. Ministry begins with the whole people of God. This means that if one were to chart it, ministry would not take place pyramid style, from the "top down." Clergy alone do not constitute the church, nor do they "do" ministry for the rest of the church. However, because we speak of the *laos,* the whole people of God in ministry together, we do not simply invert the pyramid as though ministry were constituted only from the "bottom up." Rather, both clergy and laity must *work together* in the church's ministry. To function well the church must recognize those leaders whom God has called and gifted.

To speak of representative ministry is to move away from a discussion of kind, or degree, or character that separate some from the general ministry of all. Rather it *re-*presents or brings a focus to a particular facet of ministry, as Geoffrey Wainwright explains:

> The idea is that the special or ordained ministry brings the multi-faceted ministry of the whole Church to sharp or concentrated expression in such a way that all Christians may be stimulated and enabled to exercise the Church's ministry. . . .[22]

The particular focus may vary according to the office represented. One office may focus on the Word while another focuses on the diaconal service of the church.

Lewis Wilkins cautions against the current overemphasis on the "political-jurisdictional" element of ordination which "elevates the

22. Geoffrey Wainwright, *The Ecumenical Moment* (Grand Rapids: Eerdmans, 1983), 99.

question of rights to participate with a vote . . . and makes ordination . . . more and more an admission ticket to the conference rooms and assembly halls where church power is exercised."[23]

In ordination, the Spirit of God is acting to create a new reality, a newness that is found both in identity and relationship. The ordinand responds to the church's call with vows or promises, thereby entering into a covenant relationship: that ordinand is now held accountable through the discipline of the church. The new identity of the person ordained is that of a representative of the ministry of Christ. Additionally, the ordained is given the particular authority that accompanies the designated office. Corporately, this ordering is the structure which shapes the ongoing life of the church.

The Spirit Sustains and Empowers

It is God's own Spirit which sustains the ongoing ministry and structure of the church. It is also God's Spirit which will disrupt that structure when it becomes oppressive and/or in need of renewal. In the history of the church, this has become evident through an alternating cycle of Spirit-filled event, institution to preserve this event, and new Spirit-filled event which forces the institution to change to prevent ossification.

Mortimer Arias cited as an illustration of this the seven who were elected in the early church to serve at table, so that the apostles could continue to preach the Word (see Acts 6:1ff.). But the first to be called an evangelist was precisely one of the seven, and the first one to die for preaching that Word was also one of the seven. "So the Holy Spirit was playing games with those who thought they already had the final structure," Arias wryly points out.

And the Spirit continues to sustain those who are called and ordained to witness and embody the ministry of Christ. Through them the Spirit makes visible the face of Christ so that hearts are inspired, the hungry are fed, the oppressed are freed, and new life might be given to the dying. It is the Holy Spirit that continues to give leaven so that faith and covenanted ministry remain continually new.

---

23. Lewis Wilkins, "Renewing the Office of Deacon," in *Ordination: Past, Present, and Future,* 24.

Chapter Seven

The Spirit in the Mission and Service of the Church

THOMAS HOYT, JR., AND CLYDE STECKEL

The church in the movement of the Spirit discerns the Spirit at work within it not only internally, within its own fellowship, but also in thrusting the church outward in mission and service to the world. This is clear already at Pentecost when the church, empowered by the Spirit, witnessed boldly and effectively to the gospel and demonstrated its power in service to those in need (Acts 2–3). It seems axiomatic that where the Spirit is present there is always movement toward the neighbor. Luke attests that when the Spirit moved Jesus to begin his ministry, Jesus quoted from the prophet Isaiah: "The Spirit of the Lord is upon me, because he has anointed me to bring good news to the poor. He has sent me to proclaim release to the captives and recovery of sight to the blind, to let the oppressed go free, to proclaim the year of the Lord's favor" (Luke 4:18-19; cf. Isa. 61:1). And it is by the power of this same Spirit that the church is also called and enabled to witness to God's great gift of salvation given in Christ. Thus the Spirit manifests itself as truly and powerfully in the mission and service of the church as in every other aspect of

Thomas Hoyt, Jr., teaches New Testament at Hartford Seminary, Hartford, Connecticut. He is a member of the Christian Methodist Episcopal Church.

Clyde Steckel teaches theology and psychology at the United Theological Seminary Twin Cities in Minnesota. He is a member of the United Church of Christ.

the church's life. It is this that we will examine more closely in this chapter.

The Spirit in the Mission of the Church

According to the biblical narrative, the Spirit led Jesus to proclaim the coming of the *basileia* of God, the full and effective implementation of God's reign. Later, the Spirit creates and empowers the church to herald the coming of God's new order through Jesus. But what is the relation of the church to the coming kingdom or reign of God? Jesus is presented in the Gospels as proclaiming both the presence (Luke 17:21) and future (e.g., Mark 1:15) of God's reign; but he especially stresses the urgency for his hearers to prepare to receive it and welcome it with joy. This reign or rule of God is the new order in which God's sovereignty is effectively acknowledged and made visible. It is already becoming so in Jesus' ministry, but it will be realized fully only in the future.[1] To enter into it requires a whole new way of life and relationships on the part of those who accept it, but their efforts do not bring this about. It is finally God's gracious and "mysterious" gift (Mark 4:11), which God works in them. What this implies for the church is that the church, too, lives in expectation of and witness to God's coming reign.[2] The church is not simply identical with the kingdom of God, although it shares in the power of its coming. The church is to be the Voyager of the kingdom, we might say, broadcasting its message to all who will hear.

This means that while the church and God's new order are not identical, they are nevertheless connected. Like Jesus, the church is to

---

1. On the complex relation between present and future in Jesus' sayings concerning the reign of God, see the essays in Bruce Chilton, ed., *The Kingdom of God*, Issues in Religion and Theology 5 (Philadelphia: Fortress Press, 1984).

2. Jürgen Moltmann employs the image of the church as an "exodus community" whose journey in hope attests the God of promise. See his *Theology of Hope* (London: SCM Press, Ltd., 1967), esp. chap. 5; and idem, *The Church in the Power of the Spirit* (New York: Harper & Row, 1977), chap. 3. On similar images of the church in African-American church tradition, see Major J. Jones, *Black Awareness: A Theology of Hope* (Nashville: Abingdon Press, 1971); and James H. Cone, *God of the Oppressed* (New York: Seabury Press, 1975), esp. chap. 3. See also Kortright Davis, *Emancipation Still Comin': Explorations in Caribbean Emancipatory Theology* (Maryknoll, NY: Orbis Books, 1990).

proclaim the reign of God as *coming,* as that which God ultimately intends and is working to bring to fruition. The church should see itself as the temporary, provisional, and interim means God uses to achieve this end. The church itself is not the goal toward which God moves but it is to be a community that serves to lead people toward that goal (Rev. 21:22). Thus, also like Jesus, the church must preach and teach that the coming of God's reign is the all-powerful act of God, not something we can construct by ourselves. The church cannot "build" or create the kingdom of God but is to witness to it, by sharing in its gracious coming, praying for it, suffering on its behalf, and joyfully attesting it in and to the world.[3] And also like Jesus, the church is to witness to the coming of God's reign as God's blessing and claim on the whole of life, personal, social, and cosmic. No aspect or area of life is exempt; God seeks the redemption of the creature and creation in its totality (see, for example, Rom. 8:18-25; 1 Cor. 15:25-28; Phil. 2:9-11).[4]

Furthermore, the church, following Jesus, must preach that the coming of God's reign signifies salvation for sinners and the overcoming of the powers and patterns of sin. The reign of God does not come smoothly and easily; it involves an intense struggle against all that stands in the way of and that resists the healing of creation.[5] This not only signifies a radical transformation for those outside the church and the structures of society that perpetuate and tolerate injustice, oppression, and dehumanization, but it also calls for a deep repentance and transformation of members of the church and of the church itself.[6] Thus, like Jesus, the church must proclaim the gospel in such a way

---

3. Cf. Carl E. Braaten, *The Apostolic Imperative: Nature and Aim of the Church's Mission and Ministry* (Minneapolis: Augsburg, 1985); Ignacio Ellacuria, *Freedom Made Flesh: The Mission of Christ and His Church,* trans. John Drury (Maryknoll, NY: Orbis Books, 1976); John Meyendorff, *Witness to the World* (Crestwood, NY: St. Vladimir's Seminary Press, 1987); and John R. Stott, *Christian Mission in the Modern World* (Downers Grove, IL: InterVarsity Press, 1975).

4. For more on this, see José Comblin, *The Meaning of Mission* (Maryknoll, NY: Orbis Books, 1977).

5. See the insightful discussion concerning this in Douglas John Hall, *Christian Mission: The Stewardship of Life in the Kingdom of Death* (New York: Friendship Press, 1985).

6. For more on this, see Hans Küng, *The Church* (New York: Sheed and Ward, 1967), esp. 88ff. and 150ff. See also Leonardo Boff, *Church: Charism and Power: Liberation Theology and the Institutional Church* (New York: Crossroad, 1985); and Douglas John Hall, *Has the Church a Future?* (Philadelphia: Westminster Press, 1980).

that all who hear it, both outside and within the church, hear it as calling them to a radical decision for God. This is literally a life-or-death decision. But to choose for God, that is, for life, calls for radical changes in our values, lifestyles, relationships with others, and relationships as churches. In a nutshell, it calls us to live our life as the church more fully in God's mission.

But what is this mission? And how is the Spirit active in (and also beyond) the church in it? There seem to be at least four components here that are crucial. First, the Holy Spirit is given to the church to raise up and energize the church in witness to the gospel. The Spirit is given first of all to the church, to the community as a whole, not only to individual believers (although also to them). Too often we have focused only on the gift of the Spirit to individuals and neglected to see that in the New Testament picture the Spirit is poured out on the church as a whole to make it a community of witness (for example, note the plural as well as singular meaning of "you" in 1 Cor. 3:16-17; cf. also John 20:22). The Holy Spirit creates a fellowship *(koinōnia)* that breaks down all barriers separating people and draws them into one family of faith.

Second, the Holy Spirit leads and guides the church to share the good news with others. The book of Acts is the story not only of the acts of the apostles but also the story of *the acts of the Holy Spirit who guides the church in moving out in mission*. Philip was led to meet the treasurer of Ethiopia and explain to him the meaning of Scripture (Acts 8:26-39). The apostles were led to new regions to proclaim the gospel and were often amazed at the powerful working of the Spirit (Acts 10:45) in moving beyond Jerusalem and Judea and Samaria and reaching to the ends of the earth.[7] Nothing can ultimately prevail against this missionary movement of the Spirit: social, economic, political, sexual, ethnic, and religious barriers are broken through and a new type and quality of community is created. But it is also the case that in the power and guidance of the Spirit the church has to struggle with resurgent and new forms of discrimination in changing social and cultural contexts and has to try to overcome these not only in society but also in its own life.

Third, the Spirit gives gifts of witness to people and to the church

---

7. For more on this, see Lesslie Newbigin, *The Open Secret* (Grand Rapids, MI: Eerdmans, 1978).

as a whole. The Spirit strengthens its fellowship and makes it a vital witness to the gospel. That is not to say that there will not be differences and tensions within its own life. But the church is to demonstrate the gospel also in how it handles such differences. Are these differences allowed to create party factions and divide the church and undercut its witness, or are they dealt with in a way that shows at the same time concern for truth and the unitive and reconciling power of the gospel? Paul addressed this issue in the church at Corinth, and he had a stinging rebuke for those who were attempting to fragment the church. He reminded them that there were varieties of gifts and that all these gifts were to be used for the upbuilding of the church and its witness. The Spirit gives various gifts, not simply for the personal edification of those who have them, but so that they can contribute their gifts to the community's well-being and advancement of the gospel.

And fourth, the mission of the church is sustained and renewed by the Holy Spirit. The church is not self-propelled and self-sustaining. It draws upon and lives by a power far mightier than itself. Moreover, its openness to and concern for the world, its reaching out in witness and ministry, and the power and effectiveness of its proclamation come from this power mightier than itself.[8] Because the church is shaped and moved by the Spirit which is God reaching out to the world, reaching out to those who are wandering in the dark, its own outreach is the expression of God's outreach and is sustained by it.

Mission that is sustained and directed by the Spirit will manifest this also in its methods and execution. Specifically, this would appear to require methods

> that are not impositional but dialogical, that present the gospel but also invite response and interaction;[9]
>
> that "embody" the gospel in the situation, in such ways as to implant it in the lives of peoples, rooting it critically in their cultures, traditions, languages, and ways of life;
>
> that relate the gospel concretely to the needs and well-being of people and to healing their relations with one another and the rest of creation;

8. See Küng, *The Church*, 99ff. See also Moltmann, *The Church in the Power of the Spirit*, esp. 66ff.

9. See on this Leonardo Boff, *When Theology Listens to the Poor*, trans. Robert R. Barr (San Francisco: Harper & Row, 1988).

that address not only the symptoms but also the underlying causes of human suffering and misery;

that show persistence in faith and hope and love even under duress and difficulty, as in many situations in which the church encounters pressures to conform or endures persecution for not doing so around the world today;

that show that the gospel brings redemption and healing to the whole of life, body and soul, person and society, humanity and nature;

that show that the gospel is good news not just for one segment of humanity but for all of humanity, for young and old, for poor and rich, for women and men, for minorities and majorities, for peoples of older cultures and peoples of newer cultures;

that draw people into cooperative, mutually supportive, and affirming and transforming relationships, so that their life together comes to manifest more clearly the message they proclaim;

that develop a style of leadership in which service, rather than domination, is honored and encouraged;

and that communicate more clearly and unambiguously the meaning and power of the gospel and that allow the Holy Spirit to implant and nurture it in the lives of persons, in the community of the church, and in the life of humanity.

When this occurs the church will show that it has "received not the spirit of the world, but the Spirit which is from God" (1 Cor. 2:12).

The Spirit in the Service of the Church

The servant character of the Christian community and the many servant ministries of churches are well attested in Scripture and succeeding church history.[10] The saving work of Jesus Christ, as enacted in his ministry of service and in the pouring out of his life for

---

10. Adrian M. van Peski, *The Outreach of Diakonia: A Study of Christian Service* (Assen: Van Gorcum, 1968). In addition to the classic works on this by Ernst Troeltsch *(The Social Teaching of the Christian Churches)* and Bernard Häring *(The Law of Christ),* see more recently Paulos Mar Gregorios, *The Meaning and Nature of Diakonia,* Risk Books Series No. 38 (Geneva: World Council of Churches, 1988).

others even unto death, is the ground of the church's servant ministries.[11] But it is the presence and power of the Holy Spirit that enables and guides the church in carrying out these ministries.

The church's ministry of service has taken many forms in its history, ranging from personal acts of caring to establishing large-scale institutional systems for relief of human misery, such as the more recently established Church World Service. In some branches of the church these ministries have sought to address the social and institutional causes of human suffering and worked to restructure society to make it more just, while other branches in the church have called for withdrawing from a society they perceived to be corrupt and the need for forming an alternative Christian community. Today, in many churches, working for a more just society is understood to be essential to the church's ministry of service.[12] This springs from the growing recognition that the conditions which produce poverty and oppression must be remedied along with providing immediate care for their victims.

Emphasis on the calling of the people of God to service runs throughout Scripture. It is already indicated in the calling of Abraham and Israel to be a blessing to the peoples of the earth (Gen. 12:3). It is especially prominent in the prophets (for instance, in the image of Israel, or the faithful remnant, as God's servant or "suffering servant," in Isa. 40–55). Jesus' life and ministry are portrayed as that of one "who came not to be served but to serve" (Mark 10:45) and whom the church early proclaimed to be the suffering servant spoken of in the Isaianic poems. Also, the New Testament texts present Jesus as calling his followers to be servants of one another and to follow him in a life of service. It is true that in John 15 Jesus calls his followers "friends" rather than "servants" (v. 15), but this does not contradict his instruction that they are to live in service; rather, it indicates that

11. See Emilio Castro, "Diakonia as Our Response to the Crucified Lord," in *Diakonia 2000: Called to be Neighbors,* ed. Klaus Poser (Geneva: World Council of Churches, 1987), 21-26; also, Clem J. Walters, *To Serve as Jesus Served* (South Bend, IN: Charismatic Renewal Services, 1983).

12. A point made not only by Latin American liberationists but also by many others in the world church. See *Contemporary Understandings of Diakonia: Report of a Consultation* (Geneva: Commission on Inter-Church Aid, Refugees and World Service, World Council of Churches, 1983). See also Frederick Herzog, *Justice Church* (Maryknoll, NY: Orbis Books, 1980).

this service is to be not merely compliance with a heteronomous demand but is to flow out of a deep and sincere love for Christ and for the neighbor. Consequently, the community of service is to be one in which there is equality and mutuality, and in which service affirms and does not degrade the other.

Furthermore, the Gospel narratives emphasize that it is God's Spirit which empowers Jesus' servant ministry. This Spirit which descends on or is conferred upon him at his baptism (Mark 1:12) is the power in which he carries out his ministry of healing and transforming human life (see Matt. 12:28; Luke 4:18, etc.). And it is this same creative and empowering Spirit of God, which is active in creation, history, and Jesus, which is poured out on the church at Pentecost, and which forms its life in mission and service.

That this is so is evidenced in many ways in the history of the church. One indication of it in the early Christian community was the provision it soon made for its own members who were in need: the hungry, the sick, the lonely, widows and orphans. It is less clear whether the early church extended such servant ministries also to non-Christians. No doubt, to tend to the needs of members of the growing Christian community taxed the resources of the early church to the limits; and their expectation of the imminent coming of Christ in glory gave strong impetus to preach but not to try to change the secular order. It is also not clear whether the early churches thought of themselves as "servant communities." Was the image of the servant church prominent in the self-understanding of these churches? Avery Dulles does not think it was. He argues that the model of "servant church" is a twentieth-century creation, which emerges in the Western church at a time when secularization has replaced Christian hegemony.[13] But whatever truth there may be to this, it is clear that the early Christian communities took their clues from the servant ministry of Jesus, which the Gospels show they remembered and held before them, and saw their own ministry as derivative from his (see Phil. 2:5ff.; 1 Cor. 3:11ff.; Eph. 4:17ff.).

By the beginning of the Middle Ages, hospitals, hospices, schools, and houses for pilgrims and the poor were developed by the church in exercise of its ministry of service, and the church has been engaged

---

13. Avery Dulles, S.J., *Models of the Church* (Garden City, NY: Doubleday–Image Books, 1978), chap. 6.

in developing such agencies of service even to the present day. Religious communities and orders also carried out servant ministries of various kinds.

The Protestant reform movements of the sixteenth century were concerned not only for right belief and a purification of the church's life but also for a faithful *praxis* in the relation of church and state and of concern for the neighbor. Luther's emphasis on the priesthood of all believers was intended to underscore that each believer was to serve as priest of God's mercy to others, not (as is often mistakenly assumed) that each had direct access to God and had no need of others. He emphasized also that Christian freedom was freedom for service to others.[14] Calvin, too, insisted that the Christian and the church must evidence in their lives God's gracious election and calling. If anything, the radical Reformers placed even more stress on the importance of manifesting in love and service to others faithful response to God's love in Christ and life in the Spirit.

In modern European and North American societies, beliefs about human rights, democratic forms of government, and the obligation of the state to provide for those in need have led to a secularization of many of the church's servant ministries. These have now largely become what is called "social services." Developing nations in other parts of the world have also had and are creating more governmental agencies of social help.

The church has viewed this development with some ambivalence. On the one hand, it can affirm and celebrate the growing awareness and responsiveness to social needs on the part of government and other secular institutions. At the same time, it sees that these forms of meeting social needs are often superficial, subject to corruption, discriminatory, and often do not deal with the root causes of poverty and human misery. Consequently, though the process of secularizing social ministry has been underway for over two centuries now, the church is still not clear about how it should respond to this development. Should it try to supplement secular efforts? Work to reform them? Create alternative forms of social ministry? Provide chaplains for secular institutions? Educate people with religious perspective as

14. See especially his essay on "The Freedom of a Christian" (1520), which can be found in John Dillenberger, ed., *Martin Luther: Selections from His Writings* (Garden City, NY: Doubleday–Anchor Books, 1961), 52-85.

well as practical expertise (such as agricultural and medical missionaries)? What *is* clear, however, is that an authentic social ministry must address the needs of whole persons and the relations with others in which they live their lives, and thus spiritual concerns are involved as well as issues of quality of life and the patterns and structures of the relationships of peoples in the world community. Pentecostal and charismatic movements remind the church that without the Spirit its social ministry all too easily becomes simply another form of secular "hand outs" to the needy which does not meet their deepest need.

At the same time, concern to minister to the spiritual needs of persons cannot be restricted to the "inner life" but has to do with the whole of life, that is, with the quality of life in relations with others. Thus it inevitably has to do with politics. The political dimension of servanthood means that the church must speak out and be involved in issues affecting human well-being, human "welfare" in the largest sense, as well as issues affecting the environment.[15]

One of the great achievements of the twentieth-century ecumenical movement is that it has helped the church face up to and grapple with fundamental issues of faith and their social and political bearing. More particularly for our present concern, this has meant that attention to the person and work of the Holy Spirit and its movement in the church and in the world no longer remains an emphasis only in the so-called "spirit" churches and traditions but has come to be a shared concern in our attempt to discern more clearly together as churches what the Spirit is doing among us.

The document *Confessing One Faith* is an ecumenical commentary on the Nicene-Constantinopolitan Creed of 381 that is currently before the churches for study and response as part of an effort spearheaded by the Faith and Order movement to work toward a common confession of the apostolic faith.[16] This contemporary ecumenical commentary on the creed, which is most widely used in the churches, contains a number of important statements about the Holy Spirit and

---

15. Therefore the church must be concerned about and work to correct what has been referred to as debilitating "bonds of imbalance" among peoples in the world community. See Claudius Ceccon and Kristin Paludan, *My Neighbor — Myself: Visions of Diakonia* (Geneva: World Council of Churches, 1988), 29ff.

16. *Confessing One Faith: Towards an Ecumenical Explication of the Apostolic Faith as Expressed in the Nicene-Constantinopolitan Creed (381),* Faith and Order Paper No. 140 (Geneva: World Council of Churches, 1987).

the Spirit's authorizing and empowering of the churches' servant ministries. In the document, the Spirit, which the creed refers to as "the Lord, the giver of life," is said to have spoken most clearly through the prophets. The commentary on this notes that "belief in the Holy Spirit implies that God's power is present in the world." The statement goes on to note that the presence of God in the Spirit "frees creation" and "is a power for the liberation of men and women, even from the most oppressive and enslaving forms of human sin." Moreover, as the "giver of life," the Spirit calls men and women "to respect, defend, and preserve the integrity of creation. . . ."

The statement emphasizes that the Holy Spirit gives new life in Christ as one is born anew, baptized, and received into the life of the church. Also, the Spirit bestows specific gifts *(charisms)* for "the building-up of the church and for service in the world."[17]

The description of the work of the Spirit in this ecumenical study suggests some guidelines for dealing with three issues that seem to recur in trying to understand the relation of the Spirit to Christian service. One of these issues has to do with the relation of general and specific gifts of service. Scripture speaks of two forms of servant ministry: One is the love *(agapē)* to which all Christ's followers are called, a love grounded in the very nature of God, and which is to be manifested through all the Christian's and the church's actions and relationships (see, for example, Mark 12:30-34; John 13:34-35; 1 John 4:7-12). But, second, Scripture also speaks of specific gifts of service, such as preaching, teaching, healing, "giving aid, with zeal," "acts of mercy," etc. (see Matt. 25:31-45; Rom. 12:6-8; Jas. 1:27). Too often the churches have succumbed to the temptation to rank or rate these various gifts, with motives of personal power and prestige getting mixed into theological considerations. Another way of ranking them focuses on examples of spiritual heroism — such as a Mother Teresa, a Martin Luther King, Jr., an Oscar Romero — and leaves most Christians who struggle to live faithfully in their daily lives on the sidelines as spectators to these outstanding examples of faithfulness. But if it is true that the Spirit that works powerfully in a Mother Teresa, a Martin Luther King, Jr., and an Oscar Romero is the same Spirit who is working in the lives of all other Christians (however hidden and ambiguous this may appear), then we must recognize that

17. Ibid., 65-73.

the Spirit works in a wide variety (and even diversity) of ways, and through an amazing variety of gifts of ministry and service. Recognizing and affirming this would help the churches nurture the variety of the Spirit's gifts in its members in an atmosphere of mutual support and love, without so much comparing and ranking, and without all the needless feelings of lack of self-esteem that result from trying to "live up to" or conform to an ideal model.

We can also gain some help from ecumenical discussion of the Spirit for the issue of the relation between the church's caring ministries and justice ministries. Sometimes these are viewed as conflicting. It is thought or said that those who are concerned to give immediate care for the sick, the lonely, and those suffering from marital and other problems do not see or address the social conditions and causes which underlie such problems, while those concerned for righting social structures and patterns are sometimes perceived as uncaring about the immediate needs of people. At the parish level this conflict may be played out between diaconal and social action committees, while at the national denominational level it manifests itself in tensions between chaplaincy and social action and mission boards and agencies.

The conflict is not only over mission priorities and the use of scarce resources, although it is frequently presented in this way. The basic issue is that care givers are sometimes perceived as practicing a Band-Aid approach to people's ills, while social activists are sometimes perceived as more committed to an ideology of political radicalism than a real concern for suffering people. The churches of the United States are generally tilted more in the direction of individual care ministries than in addressing social causes and conditions, although the growing numbers of homeless and hungry and declining governmental programs of aid are forcing the church to give more attention to the causes of homelessness and poverty. Still, it is largely true, as Bellah and his associates report in *Habits of the Heart,* that in the American social climate of individualism and emphasis on self-help the spiritual and psychological needs of individuals and families receive by far the larger share of the church's attention. But questions can be raised about this both scripturally and in terms of present experience. Biblically, love of God and love of neighbor are tied inseparably together, and the neighbor is one who renders aid to those in need (as the Parable of the Good Samaritan makes quite clear, Luke 10:29-

37).[18] And it is increasingly clear to us today that helping those in need must involve much more than simply providing a meal and shelter to the growing number of homeless. It must also involve working to develop affordable housing, job training and opportunities, better education, reversing the growing underclass in the cities, and improving economic conditions, among other things. The Spirit is not divided between caring and social ministries, but it is the same Spirit that works through both to make well the whole person and the whole society. Therefore these two ministries, even though they have different aims, cannot be indifferent toward each other; they are two hands of the one Spirit.

When those involved in such ministries fail to recognize this and lose touch with the Spirit, they inevitably come to experience problems of stress, frustration, and burnout. They come to realize that the needs are enormous. And they soon see that human resources of energy, sympathy, feeling, and goodwill, as well as material resources, are not sufficient. Furthermore, often there is little recognition by the church as well as by society for servant ministries. And added to this is the fact that the pay to those involved in such ministries is often lower than to those involved in other forms of ministry. Also, some servant ministries are in high-risk situations — sometimes there is the risk of physical danger; more often there is the risk of having to stand against attitudes, stereotypes, and discriminatory practices of the dominant culture and even of the church. Support groups and times of retreat can be helpful in dealing with stress and frustration. But they are not enough. The Holy Spirit provides resources of strength, wisdom, patience, persistence in well-doing, and confidence far beyond our techniques and therapy sessions. To practice disciplines of prayer, study, and worship by which the Spirit can fill our lives is to keep open channels through which we may receive the power to "keep on keeping on" in the long journey to a new and better world. If we can find ways in our churches to show the essential unity of prayer and servant ministries,[19] we will take a major step in resolving the tension between

18. For more on this, see Jon Sobrino, S.J., and Juan Hernandez Pico, S.J., *A Theology of Christian Solidarity*, trans. Phillip Berryman (Maryknoll, NY: Orbis Books, 1985). The authors go on to urge that the churches should also enter into Christian solidarity in service with the oppressed.

19. As some Latin American liberationists are pointing the way; see esp. Gustavo Gutiérrez, *A Theology of Liberation,* rev. ed. (Maryknoll, NY: Orbis Books, 1973, 1988),

those who are calling for more concentration on "spirituality" and those who believe the church must not be diverted by this from God's calling to work for justice and peace.

But more than simply diminishing this tension, a fresh attention to the work of the Holy Spirit in and through the church's servant ministries will enrich those ministries beyond anything we can imagine based on our own insights and energies.

There are many signs of spiritual renewal in the churches in the late twentieth century as well as of the activity of the Spirit beyond the churches in the world. That is why it is important that we try to see more clearly the connection between the activity of the Spirit in the church as a whole and in the church's servant ministry and the wider activity of the Spirit in the world.

116-20; and Jon Sobrino, *Spirituality of Liberation* (Maryknoll, NY: Orbis Books, 1988); and esp. Consuelo de Prado's essay in *Through Her Eyes: Women's Theology from Latin America,* ed. Elsa Tamez (Maryknoll, NY: Orbis Books, 1989). But see also Barbel von Wartenberg-Potter, *We Will Not Hang Our Harps on the Willows,* Risk Book Series No. 34 (Geneva: World Council of Churches, 1987); and Charles Elliott, *Praying the Kingdom: Towards a Political Spirituality* (London: Darton, Longman & Todd, 1985).